# Golf Courses of North Wales

## Mark Rowlinson & Peter Lees

**Published by** Sigma Leisure - an imprint of
Sigma Press, 1 South Oak Lane, Wilmslow, Cheshire SK9 6AR, England

**British Library Cataloguing in Publication Data**: A CIP catalogue record for this book is available from the British Library.
**ISBN:** 1-85058-563-6

**Typesetting and design by**: Sigma Press, Wilmslow, Cheshire

**Printed by:** MFP Design & Print

**Course Maps**: prepared by Jeremy Semmens, from originals produced by the authors.

**Cover design by**: The Agency, Wilmslow, Cheshire

**Cover Photograph:** Peter Lees, 8th tee, Conwy Golf Club, by Mark Rowlinson

**Photographs**: All other photographs are by Mark Rowlinson

# Foreword

by Tony Lewis, Chairman, Wales Tourist Board

*"Golf Courses of North Wales"* provides the authors with a rare song, hitherto largely unsung. We few who have taken on the big old trees at Northop, tried to punch sweet nine irons at blowing flags in Trearddur Bay, who have driven hard at the great Edward the First castle at Harlech from the second tee, who have wobbled while glancing over the cliff at the second at Nefyn — we have a secret which most of the golfing world does not know.

As Peter Corrigan, golfing correspondent for *The Independent*, put it, "exploring Wales in search of new golfing experiences is, even for a Welshman, like stumbling upon a row of Rembrandts in the attic."

The backcloth to golf in the north-west of Wales is Snowdonia and the mountain peaks. I have played Pwllheli, designed by James Braid and Tom Morris, but not Porthmadog, another fascinating mixture of heath and linksland. Yes, I adored Nefyn on the Lleyn, and let me tell you who plays there as often as he can — Michael Atherton, the England cricket captain, off a handicap of 10. Maesdu, the black field, was the venue of the bloody battle of Deganwy, in about 1098 AD.

I and my golf clubs have never been let loose at either North Wales or Conwy. As far as Conwy is concerned, the much-respected professional Peter Lees, is too wise to encourage a wandering chairman of the Wales Tourist Board who motors everywhere with his clubs in the boot but who never has the courage to take them out. Or maybe he saw me play in a medal round off the mat at Sharjah Wanderers or scatter the flamingoes at the Emirates in Dubai.

It astonishes many of my English friends to learn that the Welsh have got round to playing a game as sophisticated as golf. We are perceived as an up-and-under rugby nation in the South and a football dormitory of Manchester and Liverpool in the North. Few see in North Wales the finest sailing waters around Britain where a Manchester Olympics would have held its races, or the natural lie of the coastal land which drew an old Harrovian, Mr. Finch-Hatton, to lay out the Royal St David's course to match St George's in Sandwich and St. Andrews in Scotland in sea-side links appeal.

Listen to hoteliers in Wales and they will tell you that the golf product is one Wales should trumpet all over the world. Many groups come from near-Europe and build in competitions among themselves over four or five courses in a week. They are the ones who write most affectionately about Wales, our hospitality and the memories. Much depends on a golf club having a professional with a smiling face, happy assistants and a secretary who has a vision of the importance of golf to Wales and the Welsh — our image, our wealth, our friendliness.

Golf tourism is a major industry, but as far as I am concerned, I look forward to the course descriptions, the tips, the inside information which will make my 12 handicap portable and sustainable, even if I am a South Walian. I reckon, with this book in the bag, the rest is easy!

*Tony Lewis*
*Chairman, Wales Tourist Board*

# *Preface*

It must have been in the late 1950s that I heard Welsh spoken for the first time, in a little village near Porthmadog. At that time it seemed to an uninformed English boy that the Welsh language was on the point of extinction and I listened intently lest I should never hear it again. Happily the language is flourishing and should you happen to watch the members' play on almost any golf course in North Wales today it will not be long before you, too, hear it spoken - and on some courses it might be the only language you hear spoken. But you will have to ensure that it is a members' competition you watch for on any other day you will hear plentiful Midland and Lancastrian accents plus a few from farther afield as visiting golfers come to North Wales all the year round, and with good cause. On a Sunday afternoon in March I walked over the venerable Royal St. David's links at Harlech and the predominant accent of the players was clearly that of the Black Country. The name and address emblazoned on their luxury coach in a corner of the club car park confirmed their provenance. For a start they were welcome - visitors are *warmly* welcomed at almost every course in North Wales at almost any time. Secondly, they had a cracking good day out, the condition of the links in March barely different from mid-July with no temporary greens or matting tees. Thirdly, they will not have been overcharged; golf in North Wales is astoundingly good value. Finally they played their golf in incomparable surroundings. For Royal St. David's read almost any other top course in the area.

No doubt golf was played in the region long before any of today's established clubs came into being. A course at Conwy is known to have existed in the 1870s and the present club was formed in 1890 making it, arguably, the oldest in North Wales. Many of its near contemporaries are also links courses, and they include Aberdovey and Harlech, but, astonishingly, a course at Ffestiniog over 1,000 feet up in the heart of the mountains also dates from the 1890s. It disappeared between the wars but, to the delight of anyone who has played it, golf at Ffestiniog was revived in the 1970s and now provides an experience as close as any of us is ever likely to get to emulating Captain Alan Shepard's 1971 shot on the surface of the moon. This extraordinary wild landscape of lunar mountain scenery is but a few minutes' drive from Harlech, than which there could be no more archetypal traditional links. Such are the extremes of the splendid variety of golf available in this richly blessed land.

Stretching from Prestatyn in the north-east to Aberdovey in the south-west there is a coastline liberally sprinkled with genuine links of the first order. Keeping company with them are several excellent seaside courses of a rather different nature, such as Bull Bay and Nefyn, which combine the benefits of distinctly rolling heathland with spectacular marine views. In the north-east of the region can be found a number of parkland layouts which would not be out of place over the national boundary in Cheshire and two of them, Northop Country Park and Chirk, are, in their different ways, examples of contemporary challenge and style in course design. The hills and mountains, though, are never far away and they play host to one or two very adventurous courses. Here yardage charts are irrelevant with 5,000 mountain yards possibly equating with 6,500 of dry linksland. If you need proof, look no further than those two glorious and sporting outposts along Offa's Dyke, Llanymynech and Welshpool.

Llanymynech, it transpires, was one of the youthful stamping grounds of U.S. Masters Champion, Ian Woosnam. His partner when Wales won the World Cup of Golf in Hawaii in 1987 was David Llewellyn, currently Professional at Northop Country Park. They are perhaps the best known of the region's playing professionals of the present generation. Of those of earlier generations one can only be claimed partially, George Duncan. He was Professional at Conwy and Open Champion at Deal in 1920, but by the time he was Open Champion he had been sacked by Conwy for playing football on a Saturday. In those days no golf at all was played on Sundays - in 1913 three golfers appeared at Newport Police Court for playing golf on a Sunday at Rogerstone - and Sundays were *dry*! In 1930 it was necessary for Denbigh Golf Club to write to Rev. R.H. Davies of Swan Lane Chapel denying the accusation that Sunday drinking was permitted at the club.

Social trends in golf are a study in themselves. A letter to the *North Wales Chronicle* in 1913 states, "There are golf clubs in North Wales where it is avowed openly and unashamedly that no tradesman need seek to become a member, thus branding them as a lower order because of the unspeakable snobbery of the gentry and professional classes." That elitist tag has long been destroyed and King and commoner play golf side by side here. Membership fees are very reasonable, green fees exceptionally good value. Many clubs offer attractive packages to societies or visitors on holiday and juniors are readily encouraged. In North Wales people play golf for recreation; there is only a little of the business golf of the Home Counties. Unemployment in parts of the region is high and there is no way in which club committees are going to starve their less fortunate fellow-members out of golf by pushing up costs exorbitantly. There has been some movement amongst farmers to turn their land away from agriculture and into leisure (and golf in particular) but such is the nature of the terrain that development of this kind is much less frequently encountered here than in neighbouring England. Most golf clubs, then, remain member-owned, while the majority of the new ones are quite simple pay-and-play layouts providing fair entertainment for realistic green fees.

As far as Welsh natives are concerned they usually divide themselves into those from the north and those from the south. The bureaucrats have decreed that Mid-Wales is a separate entity. That is not for us! A very convenient dividing line runs east-west through Mid-Wales along the A 458 from Welshpool to the coast and we have taken this to be the southern border of our North Wales for the purposes of this book. It has allowed us to take in Aberdovey and Royal St. David's, without which no book with this title could be taken seriously. It proved expedient for Peter Lees to cover the western half of the region, while I explored the east. As a P.G.A. Professional Peter is automatically granted courtesy of the course, but he would, I know, wish to thank all those clubs which allowed him ready access to their course and to that essential background material which is so much more easily and digestably obtained in person from Club Secretaries and Professionals than solely from untold hours of digging in dusty tomes. For the most part I, too, was given courtesy of the course and, having no automatic right whatsoever to this, I should wish very much to thank all the clubs concerned and their officials for their enthusiastic support and help. Our initials at the foot of the essays make it plain who has written what. Where opinions are voiced they are those of whichever one of us wrote that article. Clearly, it has been our intention neither to conduct a witch hunt nor to indulge in the fashion for league tables. We are both immensely proud of the courses of North Wales and our aim has been to try to put before the reader enough of a description to celebrate the positive features of each course, to attract visitors to the sort of courses they particularly like (or warn them off those they dislike!), to remind resident golfers of the greatly varied fare on offer on their doorstep, and, hopefully, to give golfers something to read on the dark winter nights which will bring back pleasant memories of glorious summer days on marvellous courses. Each of us drew the maps associated with our essays and I photographed each of the courses, resulting in a small archive of around 500 colour slides covering every course in North Wales.

It would be a rare book which contained no errors. Ours is sure to have lapsed. It has certainly not been our intention that it should do so and we have taken every precaution to check and recheck the information within. Golf clubs have a great habit of remeasuring a hole or two or even rebuilding all 18 just after a book of this kind has gone to press. The descriptions and statistics are for the courses as we played them in the autumn of 1995 and spring of 1996. In each case the yardages are those from the men's medal tees allowing a direct comparison between courses to be made. Championship statistics are not, as a rule, given unless, by chance, they happen to be the same as the medal card. You simply cannot clutter the book with figures covering every possible arrangement of the course, and that is why we have retained the use of yards rather than metres, despite increasing metrication in golf.

Rules and regulations governing visitors' play at the various courses change frequently. For that reason we have given no indication of whether or not a handicap certificate may be required, if it is necessary to book starting times, whether or not you may visit at the weekend, dress codes and so on. The advice has to be to ring the club in advance. Generally speaking all clubs will try to accommodate you if they possibly can; they genuinely welcome visitors. The prospects for a round over one of the great championship links on summer weekends and bank holidays are understandably slim but if you head for the hills you will probably get a game and are unlikely to be disappointed. There are some tremendously good value packages available through local hotels, groups of golf clubs and so on and these are widely advertised in the golfing press and tourist information. In addition, many clubs hold Open Weeks or Open Days and there is no better way to play these courses nor a cheaper way of doing it! Enquire of the clubs in the early spring - these events are, not surprisingly, booked up very quickly. Having played half of these courses with the eyes of a visitor I have to say that the practice of putting in markers at 150 yards from the green is tremendously helpful, saves much embarrassment and speeds play up considerably. I am, at heart, a traditionalist and ought not to approve of such things but in an increasingly litigatious world the value of such aids and of scorecards which feature plans of the holes is considerable. Some courses, for better or worse, have taken out bunkers, thinned out their gorse, or removed blind shots. Certainly their character has changed but given the number of visitors the courses welcome in a year the positive aspect is that play is kept moving.

As a train-spotting boy I collected engine numbers and the greatest excitement was spotting the one engine in a class which had a different design of chimney or valve gear. I had no idea of the practical effects of these differences, but they attracted me for some reason of statistics. If I have learned anything from researching this book it is not to prejudge a course on its length or par-rating, the paper statistics. I am not in the pay of the British Association of Golf Course Architects but I have to say that it is abundantly clear on a number of these courses that there is a gulf of difference in the *quality* of the challenge set between professional architecture and many of the tinkerings of greens committees. Anyone can toughen up existing holes by adding bunkers, planting trees or creating lakes, but the acid test has to be that the greater challenge is complemented by greater enjoyment for golfers of all abilities, or, if you like, that if you fail to overcome the challenge of a particular hole you still enjoy the hole and the problems it sets. Penal architecture is easy, strategic architecture rather more difficult.

I doubt if W.H. Auden was a golfer for he wrote, in "It's no use raising a Shout":

> *Put the car away; when life fails,*
> *What's the good of going to Wales.*

Better, then, that the last word goes to *Golf Illustrated*, which in 1903 summed up its description of Conwy (though it could have been applied equally to any other course in this book):

> *Furthermore the surrounding scenery is of an inspiring character calculated also to soothe the savage blast of the unfortunate player who has torn up his card in despair.*

*Mark Rowlinson*
*Wilmslow*

# Contents

# Course addresses and telephone numbers

|  |  |  |  |
|---|--------|---------|-----------|
| 1 | Aberdovey | Aberdovey, Gwynedd LL35 0RT | Tel: 01654-767210 |
| 2 | Abergele and Pensarn | Tan-y-Gopa Rd., Abergele, Conwy LL22 8DT | Tel: 01745-824034 |
| 3 | Abersoch | Golf Rd., Abersoch, Gwynedd LL53 7EY | Tel: 01758-712622 |
| 4 | Anglesey | Rhosneigr, Isle of Anglesey LL64 5QX | Tel: 01407-811202 |
| 5 | Bala | Penlan, Bala, Gwynedd LL23 7SW | Tel: 01678-520359 |
| 6 | Baron Hill | Beaumaris, Isle of Anglesey LL58 8YW | Tel: 01248-810231 |
| 7 | Betwys-y-Coed | The Clubhouse, Betwys-y-Coed, Conwy LL24 0AL | Tel: 01690-710556 |
| 8 | Bryn Morfydd Hotel | Llanrhaedr, Denbigh, Denbighshire LL16 4NP | Tel: 01745-890280 |
| 9 | Bull Bay | Amlwch, Isle of Anglesey LL68 9RY | Tel: 01407-830960 |
| 10 | Caernarfon | Llanfaglan, Caernarfon, Gwynedd LL54 5RP | Tel: 01286-673783 |
| 11 | Caerwys (Nine of Clubs) | Caerwys, Mold, Flintshire CH7 5AQ | Tel: 01352-720692 |
| 12 | Chirk | Chirk, Nr. Wrexham LL14 5AD | Tel: 01691-774407 |
| 13 | Clays Farm | Bryn Estyn Rd., Wrexham LL13 9UB | Tel: 01978-661406 |
| 14 | Conwy | Morfa, Conwy LL32 8ER | Tel: 01492-592423 |
| 15 | Criccieth | Ednyfed Hill, Criccieth, Gwynedd LL52 0SB | Tel: 01766-522154 |
| 16 | Denbigh | Henllan Rd., Denbigh, Denbighshire LL16 5AA | Tel: 01745-816669 |
| 17 | Dolgellau | Ffordd Pencefn, Dolgellau, Gwynedd LL40 2ES | Tel: 01341-422603 |
| 18 | Ffestiniog | Y Cefn, Ffestiniog, Gwynedd | Tel: 01766-831829 |
| 19 | Flint | Cornist Park, Flint, Flintshire CH6 5DU | Tel: 01352-732327 |
| 20 | Hawarden | Groomsdale Lane, Hawarden, Flintshire CH5 3EH | Tel: 01244-531447 |
| 21 | Holyhead | Lon Garreg Fawr, Trearddur Bay, Isle of Anglesey LL65 2YG | Tel: 01407-763279 |
| 22 | Holywell | Brynford, Holywell, Flintshire CH8 8LQ | Tel: 01352-710040 |
| 23 | Kinsale | Llanerchymor, Mostyn, Flintshire CH8 9DT | Tel: 01745-561080 |
| 24 | Llanfairfechan | Llanerch Rd., Llanfairfechan, Gwynedd LL33 0EB | Tel: 01248-680144 |
| 25 | Llangefni | Llangefni, Isle of Anglesey LL77 8YQ | Tel: 01248-722193 |
| 26 | Llanymynech | Pant, Nr. Oswestry, Shropshire SY10 8LB | Tel: 01691-830542 |
| 27 | Maesdu | Hospital Rd., Llandudno, Conwy LL30 1HU | Tel: 01492-876450 |
| 28 | Mold | Cilcain Rd., Pantymwyn, Mold, Flintshire CH7 1TW | Tel: 01352-741513 |
| 29 | Moss Valley | Poolmouth Rd., Highfield, Wrexham | Tel: 01978-720518 |
| 30 | Nefyn | Morfa Nefyn, Pwllheli, Gwynedd LL53 6DA | Tel: 01758-720966 |
| 31 | North Wales | 72 Bryniau Rd., West Shore, Llandudno, Conwy LL30 2DZ | Tel: 01492-875325 |
| 32 | Northop Country Park | Northop, Flintshire, CH7 6WA | Tel: 01352-840440 |
| 33 | Old Colwyn | Woodlands Ave., Old Colwyn, Conwy LL29 9NL | Tel: 01492-515581 |
| 34 | Old Padeswood | Station Rd., Padeswood, Nr. Mold, Flintshire CH7 4JL | Tel: 01244-547401 |
| 35 | Padeswood and Buckley | The Caia, Station Lane, Padeswood, Nr. Mold, Flintshire CH7 4ND | Tel: 01244-550537 |
| 36 | Penmaenmawr | Conwy Old Rd., Penmaenmawr, Conwy LL34 6RD | Tel: 01492-623330 |
| 37 | Penycae | Ruabon Rd., Pen-y-Cae, Wrexham LL14 1TP | Tel: 01978-810108 |
| 38 | Plassey | The Plassey, Eyton, Bangor-on-Dee, Wrexham LL13 0SP | Tel: 01978-780020 |
| 39 | Porthmadog | Morfa Bychan, Porthmadog, Gwynedd LL49 9UU | Tel: 01766-514124 |
| 40 | Prestatyn | Marine Road East, Prestatyn, Denbighshire LL19 7HS | Tel: 01745-854320 |
| 41 | Pwllheli | Pwllheli, Gwynedd LL53 5PS | Tel: 01758-612520 |
| 42 | Royal St. David's | Harlech, Gwynedd LL46 2UB | Tel: 01766-780361 |
| 43 | Rhos-on-Sea | Penrhyn Bay, Llandudno, Conwy LL30 3PU | Tel: 01492-549100 |
| 44 | Rhuddlan | Meliden Rd., Rhuddlan, Denbighshire LL18 6LB | Tel: 01745-590217 |
| 45 | Rhyl | Coast Rd., Rhyl, Denbighshire LL18 3BG | Tel: 01745-353171 |
| 46 | Ruthin-Pwllglas | Pwllglas, Nr. Ruthin, Denbighshire | Tel: 01824-702296 |
| 47 | Silver Birch | Minafon Farm, Betwys-yn-Rhos, Conwy | Tel: 01492-680203 |
| 48 | St. Deiniol | Penrhyn, Bangor, Gwynedd LL57 1PX | Tel: 01248-353098 |
| 49 | St. Melyd | The Paddock, Meliden Rd., Prestatyn, Denbighshire LL19 9NB | Tel: 01745-854405 |
| 50 | Storws Wen | Bryn Teg, Nr. Benllech, Isle of Anglesey | Tel: 01248-852673 |
| 51 | Vale of Llangollen | Holyhead Rd., Llangollen, Denbighshire LL20 7PR | Tel: 01978-860906 |
| 52 | Welsh Border Complex | Bulthy Farm, Middletown, Welshpool, Powys, SY21 8ER | Tel: 01743-884247 |
| 53 | Welshpool | Y Golfa, Welshpool, Powys SY21 9AQ | Tel: 01938-83249 |
| 54 | Wepre | Wepre Park, Connahs Quay, Flintshire | Tel: 01244-822090 |
| 55 | Wrexham | Holt Rd., Wrexham LL13 9SB | Tel: 01978-364268 |

# Locations of the courses

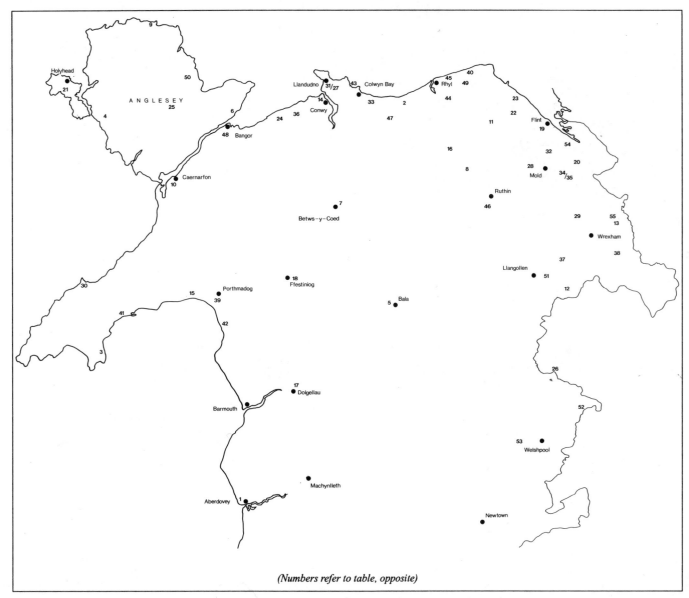

*(Numbers refer to table, opposite)*

# Golf Courses of North Wales

**An introduction by Clive Brown, Captain of the victorious 1995 Walker Cup team, winning for the first time on Welsh soil at Royal Porthcawl.**

Golf in North Wales developed in two coastal strips served in the late nineteenth century by two great railway companies. The first strip follows the Great Western Railway line from Aberdovey in the south to Pwllheli and Nefyn in the north. The second follows the London, Midland and Scottish Railway from Chester in the east to Holyhead in the west. These two modes of access to the Welsh coast allowed the influence of Royal Liverpool, one of the first three golf courses in England, to spread from Prestatyn to North Wales and all points west. Golfers from the English Midlands allowed Aberdovey, Harlech, Porthmadog and Pwllheli to flourish. Many clubs in the area are celebrating or are about to celebrate their first 100 years.

Each of the many clubs from the oldest to the youngest has an interesting place in golfing folklore and a tale to tell. The architects of the courses included Vardon, Braid and Taylor (The Great Triumvirate). The tournaments staged have included PGA Tour, Royal and Ancient, LGU and Welsh events. The players produced have included Ryder Cup, Walker Cup, Curtis Cup and Welsh International stars.

I was fortunate to start my amateur golf career at the first municipally owned golf course in Wales at Llandudno (Maesdu). Through the organisation of the North Wales Junior Golf Association the hours spent practising on the Maesdu course were put to good use in junior competitions throughout North Wales. I thought then, as I still do today, how fortunate the area is for the wide diversity of golf course available to the golfing enthusiast. From the true links courses found on the coast to the inland valley courses and the scenic, and sometimes rarefied, mountain courses, few areas in the British Isles have such variety.

Each course holds a special memory for me for, with two exceptions, I have played them all: Penmaenmawr where I played in my first competition at the age of seven and where I removed my shoes after seven holes to save the blisters; the delightful Storws Wen near Benllech, the newest course in the region, where in the inaugural competition I shot the course record - I was first out; Abersoch Invitation Day, played in October on what was then possibly the finest 9-hole course in the country with Eric and Emlyn; junior competitions at Nefyn, a course where even the best golf can be overshadowed by the majestic scenery, and at Rhos on Sea, organised by Marjorie Hartley and Jack Dodd and where we always had a wonderful tea; club matches at Llandudno (North Wales) for the Tri-ang Shield and where *LO* and *OL* could provide many a golfer's undoing - I was always nervous of saying the latter, which was probably due to my upbringing; County matches at Rhuddlan, always in immaculate condition, Llangollen hiding from the wind, and the true links of Rhosneigr where the RAF sometimes provided low level target practice; County and North Wales Counties Championships at Bull Bay, Bangor, Caernarfon, Padeswood and Wrexham.

Memories galore I have of Maesdu, played so many times as a junior that my eclectic score is 6-over twos, whose open meeting, celebrating its 75th Anniversary this year, provides member and visitor alike with competition and fellowship that is the essence of amateur golf, and all the friends and members to whom I owe so much; and now at Porthmadog, the hidden treasure of the west, where Welsh is the first language and where as a proud dad I can watch my sons develop both their golf and bi-lingual expertise.

Welsh Championships at Royal St. David's, Aberdovey,

1

Conwy and Prestatyn; two quarter-final appearances and one semi-final, and a runner-up spot in the Welsh Stroke Play provide exciting and memorable moments. Perhaps the best honour of all is representing Wales in the Home Internationals on two occasions, first as a player in 1974 and then as Captain in 1986, and as a player in the quadrangular Snowdonia Trophy all played at Royal St. David's, the only club in Wales to be honoured with a Royal Captain.

As a Welsh International, Welsh Captain and Walker Cup Captain I have enjoyed many different experiences in golf throughout the British Isles, in Europe and the USA. Golf in North Wales, for some reason, is different. The reasons for the difference are difficult to pinpoint, the difference itself hard to explain. Yet there is a difference. Perhaps it is simply that North Wales is where my home is and where I have enjoyed the majority of my golfing experiences. For me happiness is golfing competitively or with friends on one of the many golf courses of North Wales.

*Clive Brown*

# Aberdovey

*6445 yards; par 71; s.s.s. 71*

"It is the course that my soul loves best of all the courses in the world. Every golfer has a course for which he feels some such blind and unreasoning affection." These were the thoughts of the prince and father of golf writers, Bernard Darwin, at the beginning of our century. Aberdovey has continued to attract the attentions of commentators ever since, Patric Dickinson, Donald Steel, Malcolm Campbell and Peter Allen amongst them and golfers with a feel for the traditional virtues of golf have made the pilgrimage there at their prompting. For me the journey is even more evocative for I begin at Conwy, passing at first through the rolling green hills which lead to the starkness of the slate quarries at Blaenau Ffestiniog. Yet even here the rhododendrons in such profusion are mesmerising, their blazes of purple lighting up the mountainside, often literally growing from no more than a crack in the rocks. These rogue plants, however striking, came here from the Himalayas and are now almost a pest, obliterating most native vegetation in proximity. Driving eventually along the winding coast road the excitement of the golfer spying out the famous links just outside the seaside town of Aberdovey, the course on a narrow strip of land between the railway line and the sand dunes, is akin to the child getting its first glimpse of the sea and sand at the beginning of a holiday.

According to Darwin, who learned his golf as a boy at Aberdovey, the game was first played on this site as early as 1886 by his uncle, Colonel Arthur Ruck, who used flower pots to set up a 9-hole golf course. Another member of the family, Major R.M. Ruck, is credited with developing the course into a full 18-hole layout and the Aberdovey Golf Club was officially inaugurated on 9th July 1892. Fees for visitors then were 1/- a day, 2/6 per week or 5/- for a whole month.

Easter 1893 saw the first competition, attracting eleven entrants. Besides the Darwins and Rucks there were three members of the Saunders family from Stratford-on-Avon, and Messrs. Harrison and Richardson. On the eve of the event they all met in a room in the village to decide the handicaps over a whisky or two. They were over-generous to one of the Saunders family for he won the event easily with a 93. The following summer meeting generated a larger field of thirty-six, Saunders again winning with a score of 89-6 = 83 nett, 83 being reckoned to be bogey for the course at that time. In 1894 Major Ruck was mainly responsible for the formation of the Welsh Golfing Union, the senior administrative body in Wales to the present day.

The first Welsh Championship meeting graced Aberdovey the following year, in time for which a clubhouse was completed, and the green-keeper became full time on a wage of 20/- a week. Two years later it was necessary also to employ a boy as his assistant and to acquire a horse and cart. Monthly medals were introduced, but with the game new to the locals it is hardly surprising that scores varied considerably, one player gaining third position in a competition with a score of 168 in the morning and 170 in the afternoon. That, however, was in December and winter golf with the "guttie" ball cannot have been easy. In the qualifying round for that first Welsh Championship Major Ruck was the only competitor to return a score under 100, and Darwin's round of 76 in the 1894 summer meeting amazed everyone. He went on, needless to say, to international honours as a player.

By 1900 the membership had grown to 200 and the clubhouse had to be enlarged. Then in 1904 the club's first professional was appointed, one J.S. Cooper from Leatherhead. For the record Cooper was not the first professional to play at Aberdovey, Taylor, Braid, Toogood and Paxton giving an exhibition match there in 1898, Taylor triumphant with a 75. Some years later Cooper left Aberdovey to take up an appointment as Professional to the Hamilton Club in Ontario, later moving to Texas where his son, brought up in Aberdovey, became a leading player in the United States. Known as "Lighthorse Cooper" he won the Canadian Open,

*Aberdovey 3rd*

tied twice for the U.S. Open (beaten both times in the play off) and, in all, won over 30 tournaments on the other side of the Atlantic. At 91 years of age he still passes on his knowledge and skills to golfers Stateside.

During Cooper's time as Professional at Aberdovey, Darwin was asked by the committee to call in an expert to advise on improvements to the course. Darwin suggested Harry Colt and the two of them toured the course together. As Darwin wrote in his book, *Tee shots and others*, "By slow stages the first two holes

which the members had always considered rather good in their humble way, were completely transmogrified." Then in 1920 W.H. Fowler had been appointed as course architect. He commented, "Aberdovey have some very fine holes and some below the standard of a first class links and should not be found on such a fine site as you possess". Numerous changes were then made and the resulting "New" course has remained more or less the same to this day with the exception of one or two bunkers and occasional new tees. These were the days of cigarette cards and Darwin was asked by Churchmans to select a round of the best eighteen holes he knew, one from each of eighteen different courses. For his 16th he chose that at Aberdovey.

Bernard Darwin brought Joyce Wethered to play as his guest at Aberdovey in 1933. She drew the biggest crowd seen there since that exhibition match of 1898. Perhaps it is not surprising, for Darwin had already written of her as the best post-war player of either sex in Britain, and R.T. "Bob" Jones had described her as having the best swing of *any* player he had encountered. Many drives have been struck and not a few putts missed since those days, but if this seems rather a lengthy introduction it is merely to give the first time visitor some impression of the depth of tradition which informs the veneration in which Aberdovey is held by so many. It is appropriate, then, that when the Welsh Golfing Union chose to hold its Seniors' Championship at Aberdovey in 1975 it began a tradition, the championship returning every year since in September.

Just as at Harlech, you have to cross the railway line to get to the course and immediately you are struck by the air of antiquity. There used to be a great deal of nostalgia about the clubhouse, too, but, alas, the clubhouse and its aura disappeared in a recent fire. A new clubhouse is to be built. It is to be hoped something of the past era is retained.

Teeing up on the 1st it is difficult to distinguish the fairway from the rough on this crumpled corridor of land which accommodates the first three and last three holes. There is a ditch, ideally positioned across the fairway to punish a misjudged or topped second shot. Do not be fooled into thinking the course has few bunkers. This hole may have none, but there is only one more like it. With the narrow fairway of the 2nd tucked up close to the sand dunes there is every reason to play right from the tee towards the adjacent 17th fairway. The approach to the long, narrow green is relatively trouble-free.

Then comes the first par-3, a famous hole, *Cader*. It was once one of the most terrifying holes in golf, a totally blind shot over a vast sand hill with a great deal of luck about the bounce on the far side, assuming the ball made it that far. The romance of the hole was the periscope needed to see if it was safe to play. Now the hole might be described as "less blind" and the green is reasonably kind, basin shaped, but heartache can still await those today who miss or perish in one of the bunkers. Playing the 4th hole from a high tee all trouble lies to the left with towering dunes and marram grass

to grapple with. The 5th, too, is from an elevated tee, playing its full distance and cutting diagonally across this narrow parcel of land. Two ditches, numerous bunkers and humps all add to the possible strife.

The 6th, with out-of-bounds to the right and an excess of bunkers left, just short of the green, needs to be played with caution. On the 7th the ground is as flat as the proverbial pancake, a reminder that not all traditional seaside golf is played amongst the sand hills. Here distance judgement is of the very essence and there is absolutely no shelter from the wind as it whips round the side of the mountain inland. There is just a hint of right-hand dog-leg about the fairway and the greenside bunker is probably the longest I have ever seen.

The better line from the tee on the shortish par-4 8th is to the left of centre, any weak approach shot to either side invariably being punished by sand. The final hole going out may be short but it runs to a cocktail of hazards including out-of-bounds, bunkers and a ditch on the left. Neither should you underclub!

Two splendid par-4s make up holes 10 and 11, the first of which demands a well-placed drive as trouble looms down the right. The bunkers are extremely well-positioned waiting to trap a short, wayward second shot while four bunkers pin-high on the left protect the green. Just a few yards shorter, the 11th is a beauty, dog-legging to the right, and, should you miss the fairway from the tee, ditches, rough and a series of humps and hollows make the long second shot quite beastly to a gloriously shaped green.

The short 12th has a pulpit green with trouble aplenty. When played into the prevailing south-westerly wind whipping up off the Dovey Estuary I am sure a ball on the beach is not uncommon. Tees tucked high up in the dunes are a feature of holes 13 and 14. The first of these seems a never ending par-5, which I have only ever played in benign conditions. I hate to think what it is like directly into the wind. The features of the 14th come at the beginning and the end. The tee is bang in line with the edge of the dunes and a pair of bunkers collect a drive which takes too brave a line. The well-protected target is not only slick but also, as with many other greens on the links, skilfully shaped.

The last of the par-5s, the 15th, has a ditch, out-of-bounds and several more bunkers than the current course planner suggests, while the green has been redesigned fairly recently to make the pitch shot considerably more testing. And then comes Darwin's choice, the 16th, hugging the curve of the railway line and only the

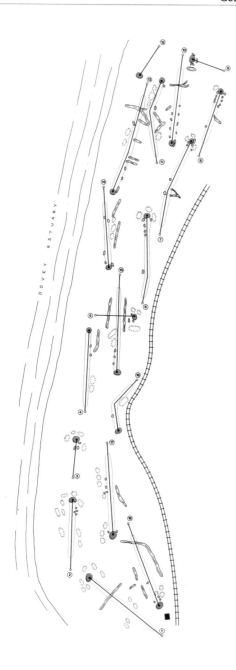

brave would choose a driver. Astute course management suggests a mid-iron to the right side of the fairway before a pitch-and-run in to a green which gathers from right to left. However it is dreadfully close to that railway line so do not leave yourself too long an approach!

Quality par-4 holes are in abundance at Aberdovey, the penultimate and final holes equal to any on the links. Both are well over 400 yards long and the 18th can be the ultimate spoiler of a good round and carefully protected score.

The layout of the holes is inevitably old-fashioned, out-and-back in the classical Scottish manner, but the setting and history are unique. The greens are, without question, year in, year out, the finest in North Wales and I am sure those eighteen surfaces of green velvet bring the visiting golfer back time and time again. No wonder Bernard Darwin's chapter on Aberdovey in his book, *Green Memories*, ends, "In short, about this one course in the world I am a hopeless and shameful sentimentalist and I glory in my shame."

*(PL)*

| Card of the course: | | | | | |
|---|---|---|---|---|---|
| 1. | 441 yards | par 4 | 10. | 415 yards | par 4 |
| 2. | 332 | 4 | 11. | 407 | 4 |
| 3. | 173 | 3 | 12. | 149 | 3 |
| 4. | 401 | 4 | 13. | 530 | 5 |
| 5. | 193 | 3 | 14. | 389 | 4 |
| 6. | 402 | 4 | 15. | 477 | 5 |
| 7. | 482 | 5 | 16. | 288 | 4 |
| 8. | 335 | 4 | 17. | 428 | 4 |
| 9. | 160 | 3 | 18. | 443 | 4 |
| Out: | 2919 yards | par 34 | | | |
| In: | 3526 yards | par 37 | | | |
| Total: | 6445 yards | par 71 | | s.s.s. 71 | |

# Abergele and Pensarn

*6520 yards; par 72; s.s.s. 71*

Speeding westwards along the ever improving A55 North Wales coast road you are bound to notice a succession of towers and turrets scattered over the wooded hillside above Abergele. They have not escaped from an extravagant film set but are parts of Gwrych Castle, an imposing look-alike from 1815 complete with attendant follies, beneath the walls of which lies the current home of the Abergele and Pensarn Golf Club, which moved here in 1968. The well-known family firm of Hawtree was employed to lay out the new course and twenty years later a purchase of further land enabled the course to be extended to just over 6,500 yards. Up around the clubhouse, beating on the castle gates, the opening and closing holes are distinctly undulating giving fine views of the surrounding hills and a comprehensive seascape. By far the greater part of the course runs over gentler parkland below.

There is nothing more inviting than the opening hole, a drive that almost cannot fail (downhill with plenty of room) and a gentle pitch up to the left to a slight ledge green. A couple of mid-irons would do the trick, but it is a handsome hole none the less, beautifully framed by trees. Immediately you cross the lane leading up to the castle and the hills give way to the parkland and life ought to be easier. Golf is rarely like that!

A mere tap with a short iron should see us onto the 2nd green, but the wind may blow us off course, possibly over the fence and out-of-bounds. Whatever the wind we will be conscious of the fence running most of the length of the 3rd hole, a par-5 curving all the time to the left and a real beggar for the persistent slicer. A number of big trees hinders the taking of short cuts while the approach has to be played up and over bunkers to a raised green. It is a strong enough hole to be rated second on the stroke index.

Longer hitters will find it difficult to resist having a go at driving the 4th. After all the hole runs downhill all the way from tee to green. Anything falling short, though, is certain to encounter the row of bunkers cutting the fairway on the diagonal just where

the trees either side close in at their most restrictive. The short 5th, too, is nicely framed in a variety of shrubs and trees and though this may be parkland golf the sea is not far distant and the wind rarely absent. A pair of mid-length par-4s, the 6th a strategic dog-leg and the 7th very straightforward, take play down to the far end of the course and one of the longer holes in North Wales.

From the medal tee the 8th is just 7 yards short of 600 but the main problem is not length so much as negotiating the trees on both sides as the fairway bends first left then right around one big tree in particular set in on the right. Even if you get on the green in three shots you will find it long, narrow and ridged. To end the outward half there is a plain par-4 requiring stout hitting as it runs back gently, but persistently, uphill.

You are allowed to play downhill on the 10th which is perhaps just as well as it is a tough proposition, Stroke 1. It is not merely sufficient to clear the big tree directly in front of the tee about 150 yards out, for you need to flirt with a pond on the right further on if you are to stand any chance of shaping an approach shot at the correct angle to hit and hold the slightly domed green. All too readily the ball shoots through into boggy ground off to the right, or comes up short in the left-hand bunker around which the putting surface is curved.

You are allowed to consolidate over the next five typical parkland holes, though you can fritter away several strokes if you tangle with the widespread bunkering fronting the elevated 11th green. The lull before the storm ends with the long approach to the 16th, the green angled, raised and stepped in such a way that only a confidently hit shot is likely to be successful.

Abergele's 17th is one of those holes dubbed "Thrombosis Hill" though in comparison with some of the holes on the more mountainous courses in this book it is gentle of its kind. In reality it is an exceedingly handsome hole, the green set on a ledge high above bunkers and even higher above the tee. Exactly how many extra clubs you should take in order to compensate for the elevation I cannot say, but, whatever the outcome of the golf, the views offer admirable compensation.

By the same token I cannot advise what the wisest approach to the 18th may be. It is the sort of hole I should not like to have to play safely in order to protect a medal card, but it *is* the sort of hole I long to attack if the match is already over and this is for a sixpenny bet. The tee is some way further up the hill behind the 17th green and the view from there is both inspiring and perplexing. The fairway races down the hillside in leaps and bounds but there is really only a very narrow gap between a group of big trees on the left and dense woodland on the right. You have to steer perilously close to those right-hand trees as the fairway leans steeply to the left, but let us hope you have conjured up the drive of your dreams then you will probably be faced with a delicate decision: you are very likely in range of the green but you are just as likely to have a hanging lie. From such a spot can you guarantee to clear the stream which has been opened up just in front of the green? Idiosyncratic it may be but the 18th hole is likely to remain in the visitor's mind for a very long time.

*(MR)*

*Abergele 18th*

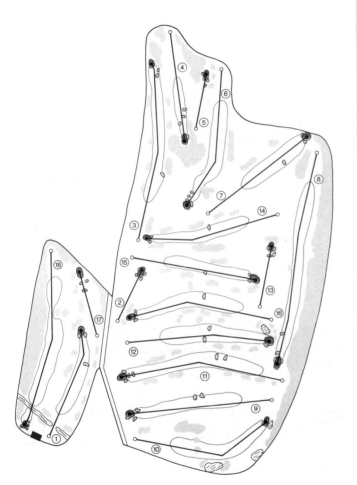

## Card of the course:

| | | | | | |
|---|---|---|---|---|---|
| 1. | 316 yards | par 4 | 10. | 413 yards | par 4 |
| 2. | 158 | 3 | 11. | 470 | 5 |
| 3. | 490 | 5 | 12. | 420 | 4 |
| 4. | 305 | 4 | 13. | 175 | 3 |
| 5. | 159 | 3 | 14. | 385 | 4 |
| 6. | 393 | 4 | 15. | 356 | 4 |
| 7. | 387 | 4 | 16. | 413 | 4 |
| 8. | 593 | 5 | 17. | 183 | 3 |
| 9. | 414 | 4 | 18. | 490 | 5 |

| | | |
|---|---|---|
| Out: | 3215 yards | par 36 |
| In: | 3305 yards | par 36 |
| Total: | 6520 yards | par 72    s.s.s. 71 |

# Abersoch

*5819 yards; par 69; s.s.s. 68*

The picturesque setting and natural harbour have made Abersoch very popular with the yachting fraternity. In spite of the seasonal influx of tourists this area towards the southern tip of the Lleyn Peninsula a few miles from Pwllheli retains its air of tranquillity and traditional nature. My visit took place in February on a morning of spring-like weather and within minutes I realised that over the years I had deprived myself of what would be a very pleasurable experience. There is an appealing aura of bygone days about the club which dates back to the 1920s and it would seem that during the winter months the members have the club very much to themselves. I felt almost an invader! Those members have something of which to feel justly proud for the back nine has

*Abersoch 18th*

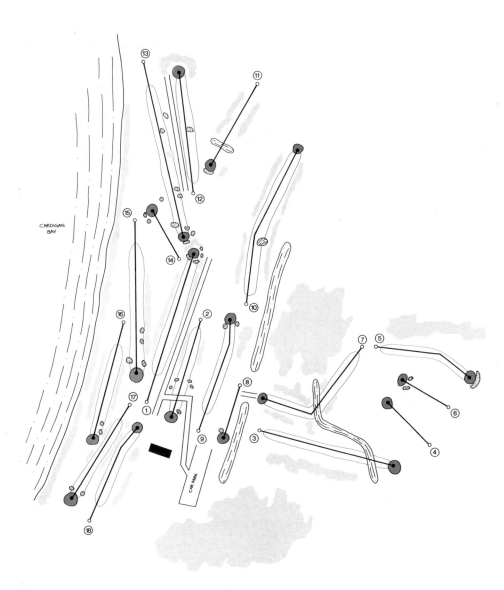

CARDIGAN
BAY

CAR PARK

enormous true links individuality and the stamp of Harry Vardon clearly there in the design. Recently nine new holes have been added, parkland and totally different in character, to make a varied and entertaining round.

Play begins with one of the meanest opening holes in North Wales with its rolling fairway and an abundance of bushes and bunkers ready to gather up an off-line second shot. Although short in yardage the par-4 2nd should not be taken lightly with its glut of traps left and right of the fairway awaiting an errant drive, a road some 50 yards short of the green, another bunker greenside and a tricky, roller-coaster green.

Leaving the links side of the course and crossing the marsh to the recently developed holes the land is in stark contrast to the original part of the course. There are several par-3s and -4s of which the most testing is the dog-leg 7th with its numerous hazards including a blind ditch spreading across the fairway at about the distance of a well-struck tee shot, while further water hazards and trees flank the right side of the fairway. Only a well-threaded second shot will be rewarded by finding the slightly raised, bunkerless green. The conservationists among us will be delighted to see that the marshland has been retained and is the breeding ground for a variety of wildlife.

It is at the start of the back nine that the course really comes into its own. The most meticulous of drives is required as a water hazard has to be avoided on the right, with out-of-bounds a further threat on that side, and more water interrupting the undulating fairway. It is an uphill climb to the bunker-free green, and I am sure sub-par scores must be few and far between, par more than satisfying. The 11th stretches almost to the maximum yardage for a par-3 and can only be described as a "toughie" despite being played from an elevated tee. The views, though, are breathtaking, the towns of Porthmadog, Pwllheli and Harlech dwarfed by the majesty of Snowdonia rising beyond. How often I will mention the Snowdon range in the course of my articles!

Teeing off on the shortish par-4 12th we begin what are, to my mind, seven links holes which equal, if not surpass, the very best in North Wales. They are steeped in tradition, unspoiled with time and a sheer delight to play over and over again. Their bunkers are spacious, revetted and manicured with the utmost care. The 13th, a fair yet testing par-5 with a rolling fairway and astutely placed traps, is a gem, while the 178-yard 14th involves a carry over rough ground, the ideal landing area being just short of the gathering green.

Stroke Index 1 is reserved for the 15th, the terrain reminiscent of Royal St. George's at Sandwich. The narrow fairway demands exacting accuracy and should you find yourself grappling with the marram grass on the steep slopes which play such a dominant rôle over these closing holes you can certainly kiss goodbye to a par. A low cottage, its windows protected with wire mesh, adds charm to the links (and a hint of the Eden Course at St. Andrews). It is a long second shot to the well-protected green and you should consider yourself fortunate if you do not have a lie which will encourage a most errant shot, but this *is* archetypal links golf.

I make no apologies for being in raptures over this wonderful back nine. The 16th is, again, full of intrigue. The dipping fairway bows round to the right leaving a lofted approach to a blind green. With two holes to go tall pine trees add to the potential pitfalls and on both holes it is the tee shot which may suffer. Although both are relatively short par-4s finding the green with the approach is not easy. A pair of bunkers only 12 steps apart protects the front of the basin-shaped green on the 17th. Standing on the 18th the setting immediately brought back memories of that great Yorkshire course, Ganton.

While it will take time for the new parkland holes to mature there is no doubt in my mind that the original holes form what was certainly the No. 1 nine-hole course in North Wales, and quite possibly anywhere.

*(PL)*

| Card of the course: | | | | | |
|---|---|---|---|---|---|
| 1. | 440 yards | par 4 | 10. | 476 yards | par 5 |
| 2. | 290 | 4 | 11. | 248 | 3 |
| 3. | 386 | 4 | 12. | 343 | 4 |
| 4. | 176 | 3 | 13. | 504 | 5 |
| 5. | 284 | 4 | 14. | 178 | 3 |
| 6. | 157 | 3 | 15. | 454 | 4 |
| 7. | 404 | 4 | 16. | 351 | 4 |
| 8. | 145 | 3 | 17. | 326 | 4 |
| 9. | 319 | 4 | 18. | 338 | 4 |
| Out: | 2601 yards | par 33 | | | |
| In: | 3218 yards | par 36 | | | |
| Total: | 5819 yards | par 69 | | s.s.s. 68 | |

# Anglesey

*6300 yards; par 70; s.s.s. 70*

That popular song *Trains and Boats and Planes* from the mid 1960s, written by that magical songwriter, Burt Bacharach, always springs to my mind when I visit this course where these three forms of transport are very apparent. The London-Holyhead railway line divides the course, a river meanders through the 18th hole and the planes on their exercises from R.A.F. Valley soar overhead. In fact in the early 1940s the Ministry of Defence compulsorily purchased the six best holes on the course. The golf course lies about a mile from the pleasant seaside resort of Rhosneigr, with its long stretches of sandy beaches on the west coast of Anglesey.

The forming of the Anglesey Golf Club was the work of two Englishmen in 1914: C.H. Palethorpe (famous for sausages) and James Ravenscroft. Harold Hilton, the great amateur golfer from Hoylake, was brought in to advise on the formation and layout of the course (and how often we shall encounter Hilton's name and the influence of the Royal Liverpool Club within this book!).

Play opens up with a fairly long par-3 with out-of-bounds flanking its right side precariously close to the green, and out-of-bounds again looms close on the next hole, especially for the drive, the fairway doglegging slightly left. The 3rd, with its narrowing fairway around the drive's landing area poses quite a problem for the following stroke to a blind green. Anyone not familiar with the course would be advised to take a leaf out of the tournament golfer's book and walk up to the ridge running across the fairway to check

**Anglesey 4th**

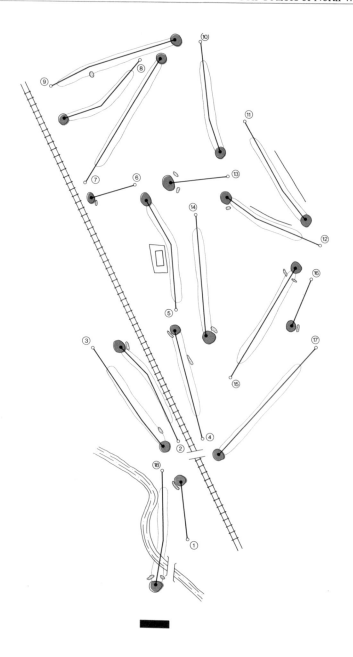

out what would appear to be a rather deceptive yardage.

Access to the rest of the golf course, bar the 18th, is through a tunnel under the railway revealing an expanse of land of very different texture and appearance from that of the opening holes. At first sight the whole area appears completely flat but, as we shall see, a number of holes have fairways which contradict this. The 4th fairway, for example, looks like a mass of mini-craters. Flat lies for the approach shot to the green are few and far between. It can also sometimes be difficult to differentiate the fairway from the rough on the holes on this side of the railway, very much in the nature of seaside golf. The dogleg 5th, with out-of-bounds to the left tends to force the drive out to the right-hand rough which is made up of sporadic clumps of marram grass and is considerably more difficult to play out of than other types of grasses. There will be plenty of this grasping stuff here at Anglesey.

A glorious short hole heading towards the railway line follows with a mass of undulations to the right of the green and a craftily placed pot bunker to its left. Its long, narrow green with its subtle borrows is typical of many greens on this course. The 7th is the first par-5 and is as straight as a die. Keep the shots in the same vein and few problems should occur. The 8th with a right-hand bend in the fairway and a profusion of the dreaded marram grass ready to clutch an errant drive to the right is a force to be reckoned with.

The last hole on the front nine has changed in numerous ways over the years. What used to be the hole's main feature, a huge fairway bunker, has been allowed to diminish to almost the size of a pot bunker, and I am pleased to learn that it may be restored to its former glory in the not too distant future. An innovation several years ago was to build two peculiar and unnatural looking mounds around the fringes of the green. If they were replaced by sand traps I feel it would make for a much fairer yet equally testing hole.

The 10th, 11th and 12th are all dogleg holes with out-of-bounds and a considerable amount of gorse to contend with. The 11th has, yet again, an uncharacteristic mound by the right side of the green – another spot crying out for a traditional bunker. On first glance the 13th appears to be a fairly simple short hole. May I suggest closer attention is paid to the fact that a bunker left of the green is cleverly hidden by a mound on the same line? Another bunker front right of the green makes the target just that little bit more difficult to hit.

The 14th, a long two-shotter, is all about keeping the ball in play. There is no particular line to take from the tee, but the second shot must avoid a left-side trap which is awkwardly placed as it is not quite green-side. Another couple of powerful smites will be needed on the next hole but, as we all know, in a bid to create power off-line shots are often produced. A mixture of tough rough, bunkers and gorse awaits a stray shot.

After playing the short 16th I walked to the 17th hole, its fairway possibly wide enough to land a *Jumbo*, and three *Harrier* jets ripped through the sky from the neighbouring R.A.F. base and within seconds were mere dots zooming over distant Snowdonia.

What would appear to be a relatively simple par-5 is very different if played into the prevailing wind.

Proceeding under the tunnel to the 18th it is time to leave this mainly unspoiled natural golfing terrain (reminiscent in parts of Royal North Devon at Westward Ho!) and long may it remain like this! The ultimate hole is the best on the course, though. Having to drive over the edge of the winding river and be faced with it yet again full on for the second shot to an uphill green is enough to make one's hair curl. So ends the round on one of the driest and best all-year-round courses in North Wales.

*(PL)*

| Card of the course: | | | | | |
|---|---|---|---|---|---|
| 1. | 199 yards | par 3 | 10. | 398 yards | par 4 |
| 2. | 372 | 4 | 11. | 385 | 4 |
| 3. | 377 | 4 | 12. | 371 | 4 |
| 4. | 362 | 4 | 13. | 196 | 3 |
| 5. | 360 | 4 | 14. | 402 | 4 |
| 6. | 158 | 3 | 15. | 418 | 4 |
| 7. | 485 | 5 | 16. | 166 | 3 |
| 8. | 380 | 4 | 17. | 490 | 5 |
| 9. | 412 | 4 | 18. | 369 | 4 |
| Out: | 3105 yards | par 35 | | | |
| In: | 3195 yards | par 35 | | | |
| Total: | 6300 yards | par 70 | | s.s.s. 70 | |

# Bala

*4962 yards; par 66; s.s.s. 64*

Llyn Tegid (Bala Lake) is four miles long, the largest natural lake in Wales, and Bala town stands at the eastern end of it, a splendid centre from which to tour Snowdonia and Mid-Wales and well-known to enthusiasts of water sports and fishing. It is less famous as a golfing resort but golf there *is* of a rigorous, upland sort with inspiring vistas from the course when the weather is kind.

The original 18-hole course was founded in 1909, situated 1½ miles out of the town on the banks of the River Dee. In later years it moved from the lowlands and became a 10-hole circuit on uplands above the town, designed by Fred Collins, the professional at the North Wales Club. The yardage may seem short and, as is so often the case on moorland courses, there are no bunkers, but the greens are smaller than most of us are used to and humps and hollows here are the real things!

Over the years I have so often been told of the daunting start to Bala, an uphill short hole. None of my words is sufficient really to describe what I discovered when at last I encountered it. Quite simply it is the most formidable par-3 I have ever played, but at

**Bala 4th**

least you only have to play it once. Be reassured! The 'huffing and puffing' is well worthwhile as the course and the most spectacular views you could wish to encounter unfold. The focal point is Bala Lake, a glistening jewel in the valley. It is ringed with range upon range of mountains separated from each other by further deep valleys, the Arennigs, the Berwyns and the Arans leading towards Cader Idris. The eye is drawn to this most undisturbed part of the land constantly, particularly from the 4th and 5th tees. Rocky bluffs emerge from the fairways themselves from time to time, especially on the 8th, a par-3 of 200 uphill yards. (When once your ball has encountered one of these rocky bluffs you will take every precaution to prevent its ever happening again!)

The last hole is a joy, the only genuinely short par-3 on the course, and, in the way the ten holes are deployed, encountered only once. It is played from an elevated tee to a green seemingly hundreds of feet below, protected by trees and the out-of-bounds which runs to the left and rear of this elusive target. So end 4,900 yards of visual delight and pure golfing fun.

*(PL)*

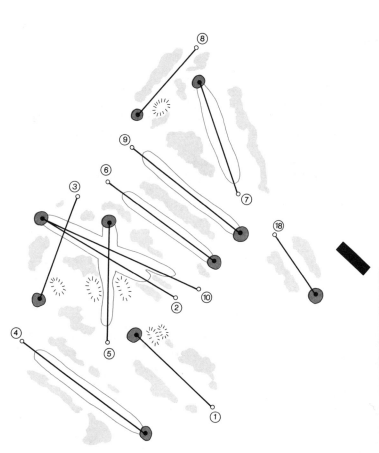

| Card of the course: | | | | |
|---|---|---|---|---|
| 1. | 231 yards | par 3 | 10. 368 yards | par 4 |
| 2. | 355 | 4 | 11. 241 | 3 |
| 3. | 241 | 3 | 12. 344 | 4 |
| 4. | 344 | 4 | 13. 278 | 4 |
| 5. | 278 | 4 | 14. 300 | 4 |
| 6. | 300 | 4 | 15. 260 | 4 |
| 7. | 260 | 4 | 16. 200 | 3 |
| 8. | 200 | 3 | 17. 304 | 4 |
| 9. | 304 | 4 | 18. 154 | 3 |
| Out: | 2513 yards | par 33 | | |
| In: | 2449 yards | par 33 | | |
| Total: | 4962 yards | par 66 | s.s.s. 64 | |

# Baron Hill

*5556 yards; par 68; s.s.s. 66*

Baron Hill is situated on the hilly western slopes of the Menai Straits on the fringe of Beaumaris, a most untypical Welsh seaside resort with its stretches of seafront lawns, Georgian architecture and Victorian and Edwardian villas. Beaumaris has a wealth of historical riches. The castle which dates back to 1295 is said to be the finest of Edward I's fortresses. Certainly it is the most complete and, in certain respects, the best designed of them. Opposite the castle stands the court house which was built in 1614, remains in its original state and is still used for its original purpose. One guidebook describes it as "very interesting if you are unfamiliar with such buildings"! Then for the unfortunate there is the jail of 1829 with its work rooms, exercise yards and soundproofed punishment room.

Golf was played at Beaumaris in the 1880s on a private course owned by Sir Richard Williams-Bulkeley, the 12th Baronet (1862-1942), which later became the Baron Hill Golf Club as we know

**Baron Hill 6th**

18

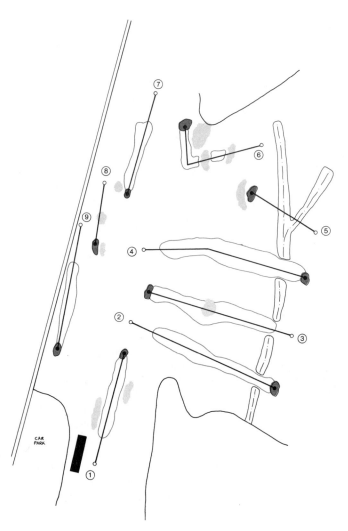

it today. This finely manicured 9-hole course with its occasional gorse bushes and rocky outcrops calls for precise judgement, no more so than on the first drive of the round played adjacent to the newly appointed clubhouse. Holes 2, 3 and 4, all of similar length, run virtually parallel to one another, two downhill and one up. There is no escaping the presence of the meandering brook which plays its part on all three holes as it does also on the well-designed par-3 5th hole.

There are few courses which do not leave a particular hole embedded in one's golfing mind and here it is the 6th, an acute dog-leg right calling for pin-point accuracy of length and direction. Should one miss out, bushes, rocks or trees can spell disaster. Next comes a fairly straightforward par-4 followed by the par-3 8th which is played from an elevated tee.

I am sure many a woeful tale has been told after leaving the 9th green. Although not a very long hole, out-of-bounds flanks the right side of the fairway every inch of the way. Holes have been re-aligned and improved and a new club house erected after the old one was ravaged by fire some six years ago, yet the course still retains the same charm and general features as the original laid out by our Victorian ancestors over a hundred years ago.

*(PL)*

## Card of the course:

| | | |
|---|---|---|
| 1. | 293 yards | par 4 |
| 2. | 413 | 4 |
| 3. | 399 | 4 |
| 4. | 427 | 4 |
| 5. | 185 | 3 |
| 6. | 321 | 4 |
| 7. | 273 | 4 |
| 8. | 152 | 3 |
| 9. | 315 | 4 |
| Out: | 2778 yards | par 34 |
| Total: | 5556 yards | par 68   s.s.s. 66 |

# Betwys-y-Coed

*4954 yards; par 64; s.s.s. 63*

Betwys-y-Coed golf course has a dramatic setting on the floor of a steep valley hemmed in by forested slopes within the Snowdonia National Park. Alongside the course the Conwy and Lledr rivers merge: an ideal spot to relax with rod and line and to take advantage of this marvellous salmon run. One of the most famous sights in the town is the cast-iron Waterloo Bridge, designed and built in 1815 by Thomas Telford to carry the A5 across the River Conwy, and tourists in thousands flock to the Swallow Falls a few miles upstream and a splendid spectacle the falls are after rain.

Golf was played on the present site from 1912 along with tennis, croquet and bowling but the golf was abandoned in 1923. It was not until 1971 that discussions took place to re-establish it and 1977 saw the opening of the present 9-hole course which is on level ground throughout.

Play opens up with a relatively straightforward par-4 and then the dog-legged 2nd with trees to its left and a cunningly placed bunker on the right of the fairway calls for an accurate tee shot. The 4th, too, is dog-legged to the left, aptly named *Conwy*, and again requires a well-positioned drive as the odd clusters of trees can play their part in accumulating a high score.

The most testing of the three consecutive par-3s is the 5th with its green set beyond the overhanging branches of numerous tall trees and although hole 6

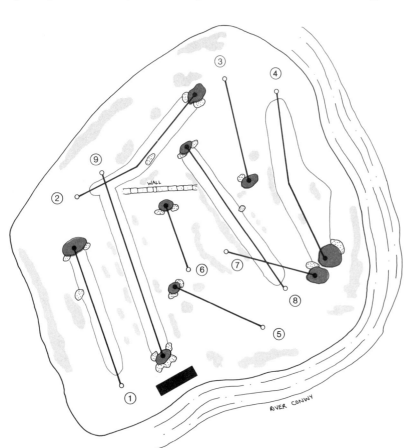

*Betwys-y-Coed 2nd*

is the shortest on the course any over-clubbing will see the ball careering into the stone wall only a few paces behind the green.

The 8th hole, tree-lined down the left and with more trees placed spasmodically on the right, plays deceptively long. That leaves the last hole, the course's longest and most testing, necessitating perfectly sized-up approach play because of a large bunker at the back of the green. Alternative tees for the second nine holes give variety and a most pleasant day's play.

*(PL)*

### Card of the course:

| | | |
|---|---|---|
| 1. | 299 yards | par 4 |
| 2. | 315 | 4 |
| 3. | 215 | 3 |
| 4. | 344 | 4 |
| 5. | 208 | 3 |
| 6. | 149 | 3 |
| 7. | 189 | 3 |
| 8. | 371 | 4 |
| 9. | 387 | 4 |
| Out: | 2477 yards | par 32 |
| Total: | 4954 yards | par 64    s.s.s. 63 |

# Bryn Morfydd Hotel

*5660 yards; par 70; s.s.s. 67*

They say that it is cheaper for a Japanese golfer to fly over to Scotland, stay at Turnberry, play the Ailsa Course, and fly home again than to play a single round on one of the best courses around Tokyo, if you can play there at all. An image persists that golfing hotels are the preserve of the super rich: The Homestead, Banff Springs, Gleneagles, Pinehurst and so on. It was, then, both reassuring and a welcome surprise to find that golf at Bryn Morfydd does not necessitate a second mortgage. In fact these are some of the best value green fees anywhere.

The hotel has been in existence for many years, enjoying a verdant hillside location south of Denbigh overlooking the Clwyd Valley and the whole Clwydian Range up to Moel Fammau. In time it ran to a 9-hole par-3 course designed by Peter Alliss and David Thomas, a wonderful asset and a serious test, but not in itself likely to draw golfers from far and wide to stay at the hotel for its golf alone. When Duncan Muirhead took over as proprietor he set about the design and construction of a full 18-hole layout. He and his Director of Golf, Colin Henderson, hit hundreds of golf balls over fields, through woods and up and down mountains in search of the layout which would make the best use of the existing geography, with the least felling of trees or earth moving, and within a budget which would keep the cost of playing the course within reach of all golfers. They incorporated a little of the Alliss-Thomas course into their own but by building 18 new holes they now have a full 27 holes between the Duke's and Duchess Courses. This allusion to the nobility (or to the Woburn courses, if you like) does not demand a king's ransom and there are all sorts of attractive packages available offering free golf to hotel guests and there are frequent residential golf schools. There is also a playing club with its own constitution and facilities.

The Duke's Course climbs over the hills and meadows behind the hotel and many of the greens follow the natural contours of the land implying that you need a better approach game than mine to stop the ball on a downhill green at the end of a long descent. There are holes, too, on which partners would be advised to act as forward look-outs for each other as shots are played blind over hilltops, but it is a fair price to pay for the expansive views and (noisy) company of the many pheasant roaming the course.

At 273 yards the 1st hole is short for a par-4 but it climbs steeply. It does mean, though, that you will want to try to drive the green on the parallel 2nd, downhill all the way and with only a single bunker beyond the gap in the trees which it is essential to find. A long par-3, backed by handsome trees, comes next, more or less on the level, but the green is not easy to find with a narrow entrance between bunkers. Unusually it is rated as Stroke 3, and the second stroke is taken on the 4th, a short par-5 but a birdie proposition only to those who can drive far enough along the sloping fairway to see round the end of the trees towering on the right. It is still a substantial hit up a steep hill, over a cross-bunker, tight through the trees, to find the green, and just the sort of hole on which it is all too easy to fritter away any number of silly shots.

Two open meadowland holes then allow you to get your puff back, the 5th mischievously tempting you to dice with out-of-bounds as you try for the awkwardly angled green. The short 7th is named *Broomieknowe*, bringing to mind a course a few miles south of Edinburgh, and the view from this tee could well distract you from the business in hand, namely taking sufficient club to climb to the green. Slice the ball and you clear a hedge, draw it and you can be in all sorts of trouble down the hill to the left. The 8th, a short par-4, takes play out onto a fourth sector of the course, rolling meadowland with occasional trees being used to strategic effect. On this hole, for instance, you simply have to find the gap between two of them from the tee. This is one of those downhill approaches which is difficult to judge. An attractive par-3 into a woodland corner completes the outward half.

There has been little length so far, only 2411 yards from the very back. The back nine is 800 yards longer and a very large part of that comes on the monstrous 10th. From the medal tee it is 617 yards long, beginning with a huge slog uphill to the point at which the fairway turns abruptly right and on over the crest of a hill before running in to an exposed green with a crafty dip in front. From the yellow tee the hole is shorter by more than 100 yards but still no sinecure because from the tee you are, nevertheless, obliged to find that same spot where the fairway turns right. A long strip of netting to protect those putting on the 8th green suggests that the natural route of the hole lies further to the right.

A big drive on the 11th sees the ball at the crest of a hill in a gap between a tree and the remains of a hedge and from there it is not too hard to find the green, but many who made less distance will be playing their second shots blind over the summit. *The Funnel* is the name of the par-5 12th and it has the makings of a memorable hole. The drive is out over a big tree, as far as possible in order to take full advantage of the generous downslope, the

memorable thing being the sight of the ball soaring out over the tree against a most scenic backcloth. In summer many of us will have no difficulty running the ball on down the hill to be on or around the green in two.

As surely as you go down a hill so you must return up it, and in golf that is the hard bit. The first hole on the climb back is pretty but perfidious. Some may fancy their chances of hitting a big draw round the corner but the penalty for failure is all too visible with an impenetrable jungle in wait on the left. Those who decide on the conservative route should try to place their tee shots in such a place that the pitch can be made into the slope of the green. I can see no way of approaching the green on the high side and surviving! The 14th demands local knowledge as it is effectively blind over a shoulder of hill to all but the tallest of golfers (or those who still have sufficient energy to jump in the air). The name *Oh No!* on the scorecard may be unusual but it is entirely appropriate if you attempt to carry the pond lying between you and the green on

*Bryn Morfydd 18th*

23

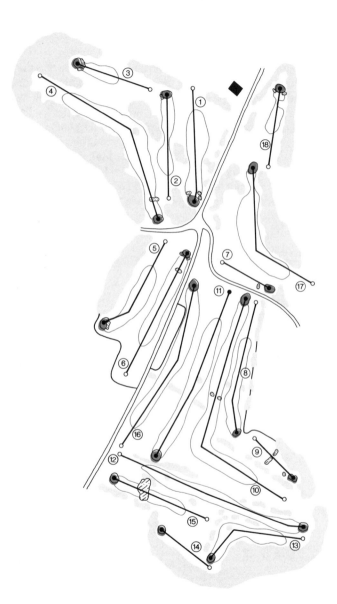

the direct line on the 15th. All too frequently those who aim to play short of the water find that they have completely misjudged the distance and have trickled in despite their best endeavours.

The 16th appeals immediately with a narrow drive through a gap needed to set up an approach which swings downhill and slightly left to another green which is very hard to hold from afar. If that is hard to hold, I reckon the 17th green is pretty well impossible unless from below – and that was how this three-level green was originally meant to be approached (a vestige of the Alliss-Thomas original). It is possible, if you get your angles exactly right, to drive this green, the fairway corkscrewing down to the right after a blind tee shot. The final part plunges down between trees and those who know what they are doing play modestly from the tee in order to leave their ball on a relatively gentle slope from where they hope to land the pitch at such a spot that the ball trickles onto the green rather than bounding through irrepressibly. The 18th continues the descent, playing shorter than the card suggests but the eye almost certainly fails to notice a hollow in front of the green which, it is threatened, may one day be filled with water. Make sure you leave time to try the par-3 Duchess Course. It is handsome, fun and not as easy as you might think!

(MR)

| Card of the course: | | | | | |
|---|---|---|---|---|---|
| 1. | 273 yards | par 4 | 10. | 617 yards | par 5 |
| 2. | 254 | 4 | 11. | 437 | 4 |
| 3. | 199 | 3 | 12. | 508 | 5 |
| 4. | 478 | 5 | 13. | 268 | 4 |
| 5. | 272 | 4 | 14. | 162 | 3 |
| 6. | 334 | 4 | 15. | 259 | 4 |
| 7. | 139 | 3 | 16. | 433 | 4 |
| 8. | 326 | 4 | 17. | 367 | 4 |
| 9. | 136 | 3 | 18. | 198 | 3 |
| Out: | 2411 yards | par 34 | | | |
| In: | 3249 yards | par 36 | | | |
| Total: | 5660 yards | par 70 | s.s.s. 67 | | |

# Bull Bay

*6217 yards; par 70; s.s.s. 70*

Bull Bay is one of three 18-hole courses on the island of Anglesey (Ynys Mon) and probably the most rugged. It is Wales's most northerly course situated about 1½ miles from Amlwch. The course lies on a plateau which stretches almost to the edge of the rocks bordering a deep coastal inlet.

I am a firm believer that golf courses do not have to be immoderately long to be challenging and Bull Bay easily satisfies my criterion. Over half the greens have to be approached from fairways which are below and numerous drives are played from elevated tees. Above all there is the guile of Herbert Fowler, that remarkable golf course architect whose best-known testament on this side of the Atlantic is the Old Course at Walton Heath on which, so to speak, he cut his teeth. Yet it is perhaps on some of his shorter, less famous layouts, such as Beau Desert, Delamere Forest and Bull Bay that one can appreciate his talent for extracting the best from a given site and his genius with the short par-4.

A very recently rebuilt 1st tee enhances a testing opening hole with its lofty green which is possibly one of the most difficult to play on the course. As with the 1st hole, a wayward drive on the 2nd calls for three off the tee. The ideal line is on the right side of the fairway, thus giving a clear view of the green. The longest of the par-3s, the 3rd, with its slight ravine can cause despair without the assistance of a south-westerly.

I can recall – only a few years ago – the course having less than a handful of bunkers although more have been added since, including a number on the 4th, but there are still fewer than a score in all. One suffices on the 170-yard 5th, quite a baffling hole with a smattering of rocky outcrops to the right and a right-to-left sloping green which demands a precise putting touch. Just 40 yards longer than the minimum suggested length for a par-4, the 6th might seem relatively simple but this is not the case. A hearty drive is required in order to carry onto the plateau of the fairway. Then the pitch must be tossed up well to find the blind green.

The next, a most demanding par-4, fully justifies its Stroke Index 1 with its abundance of trouble on the left side. The second shot from a low-lying fairway, if hit slightly to the left of the green, will be ensnared in a solitary bunker. On the 8th the high tee to a downward-sloping fairway tends to flatter the drive provided the humps, hollows and thick rough to the right are by-passed. A well-aired fairway wood shot with the help of the prevailing wind leaves little more than a lob to the green. Teeing off close to the roadside for the last hole on the front nine makes for a drive to the depths and an approach to the heights. The ups and downs of this "o so sporting" hole make club selection and accuracy the ultimate test. Another rocky outcrop and trouble to the right of the green can cause quite a mid-round crisis.

The homeward nine begins with the premier par-3. With all of the large, sloping green on view and the prevailing wind unlikely to help it is readily apparent why there is so little room for error. Then it is not only the tee shot on the 11th, still up on the high ground, which can prove problematic. It is wise to do your homework before playing the second shot as there is a slight valley to negotiate and anything played left of the green will be severely punished by a gorse-clad minor precipice.

Looking back over the first eleven of Herbert Fowler's holes it seems few changes have been made over the years. In contrast, numerous alterations have been made to holes 12, 13 and 14, the latter a most challenging down-dale and uphill dog-leg left heading up towards the roadside. After a walk round behind the 8th green what an inviting tee shot is in prospect down the fast-running 15th fairway and the last of the par-5 holes but, as with the early holes on the course, out-of-bounds lurks down the right side! Given a successful drive, the second shot, played to a fairly wide uphill fairway, will prove beneficial if played right of centre leaving an open view of the green for the approach shot.

After playing the pleasant par-3 16th, the penultimate hole,

*Bull Bay 18th*

with a fine recently reconstructed tee, although bunkerless, is somewhat hazardous with gorse to the right and even more to the left. It is a tricky dog-leg hole and it is far wiser to play it with caution than to try to cut corners.

Bull Bay is very much a thinking man's course with its tremendous natural terrain. Prior to standing on the 18th tee there has been little opportunity to enjoy the glorious views in which golfers have been revelling since the course was first played in 1914. From here a good length of the coastal area can be seen and on a clear day the Isle of Man and Cumbrian hills are in view. To the right is the impressive Snowdon range. This final hole, which has a majestic new club house overlooking the green, plays a little shorter than the card's suggested yardage, but if a little fatigue has set in beware of the two bunkers on the right side of the fairway waiting to gather a weak approach shot.

Bull Bay, when played in benign conditions, with its rolling fairways and cleverly laid out greens, offers a fair challenge to golfers of all standards.

*(PL)*

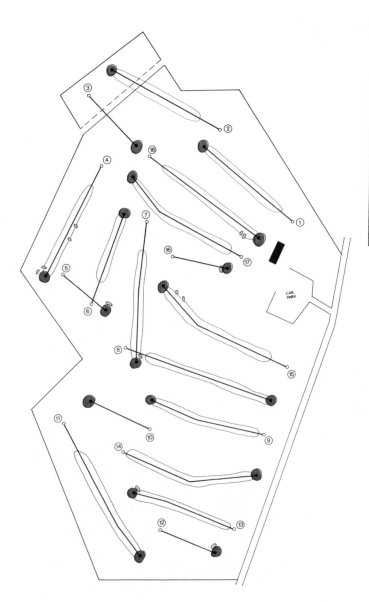

### Card of the course:

| 1. | 363 yards | par 4 | 10. | 195 yards | par 3 |
|---|---|---|---|---|---|
| 2. | 390 | 4 | 11. | 485 | 5 |
| 3. | 220 | 3 | 12. | 197 | 3 |
| 4. | 379 | 4 | 13. | 332 | 4 |
| 5. | 175 | 3 | 14. | 425 | 4 |
| 6. | 290 | 4 | 15. | 486 | 5 |
| 7. | 423 | 4 | 16. | 171 | 3 |
| 8. | 475 | 5 | 17. | 425 | 4 |
| 9. | 340 | 4 | 18. | 446 | 4 |

| Out: | 3055 yards | par 35 | |
|---|---|---|---|
| In: | 3162 yards | par 35 | |
| Total: | 6217 yards | par 70 | s.s.s. 70 |

# Caernarfon

*5891 yards; par 69; s.s.s. 68*

It was a dark and dismal November morning when I set off down the A55 to Caernarfon. By-passing the town and turning right off the A487 I drove down a country lane for a couple of miles which at a point ran alongside the River Seiont with its abundance of sailboats dwarfed by the imposing sight of the mighty Caernarfon Castle, best known of Wales's many mediaeval fortresses, a World Heritage listed site, designed to serve as a royal palace and seat of government as well as a military stronghold. The town of Caernarfon became known to the world in 1969 when the Investiture of the current Prince of Wales took place.

On arrival at the club I was reluctant to leave the warmth of the car and step into a bitterly cold wind. With an exchange of *Bore da!* to a solitary member of the green staff I made my way up to the 1st tee on this dog-leg left par-4. In kinder weather this tee gives

**Caernarfon 15th**

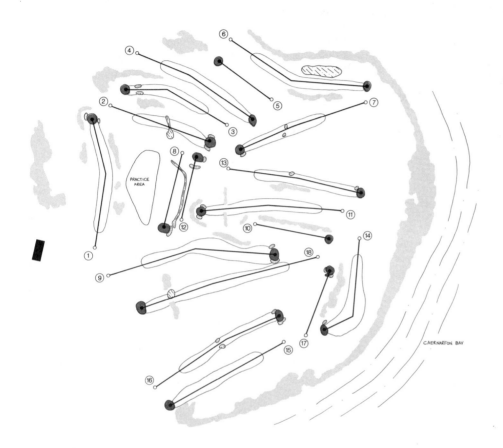

CAERNARFON BAY

*wen* (The Oak) a sharp dog-leg to the right, is the 4th. Any ball played to the right of the ditch separating this hole from the 3rd is out-of-bounds. The 6th hole, *Dwlch-y-Coed* (Gap in the Wood), another severe dog-leg, but this time to the left, plays its full length. One of the reasons for this is that the ground is relatively soft under-foot and there is very little roll on the ball. A smattering of trees borders the right side and a lateral water hazard runs down the left of the fairway.

The second of the par-3s, the 8th, takes you across *Pont Bill* (Bill's Bridge), Bill having been Captain in 1988-9. A downhill run in to the large green enables the hole to be played shorter than its 200 yards. A solitary greenside bunker is well-placed to gather any shot pulled to the left.

*Y Craig* (The Rock), with its tee perched on high ground, begs for a well-placed tee shot to the narrow start of this rich parkland fairway. A high bracken-clad embankment running parallel with the fairway can bring grief to any wild shot left. The well laid out Mackenzie green with its attendant bunkers necessitates a skilful touch.

A neat and spacious tee on a 200+ yard par-3 sets up the start of the back nine. A wall and hedgerow span the full length of the hole to the left, the higher side of the fairway. The seaward outlook here is a splendid match for the mountain views elsewhere on the course. Looking from the tee on the 11th, however, the hole appears relatively straightforward, but the second shot played to a green low down can encounter problems as the fairway narrows considerably just short of the approach to the green. The Snowdon range is a glorious backdrop for the 12th hole, *Mynydd Mawr* (Big Mountain). Playing slightly uphill a bunker some 30 yards short

fine views of the mountains of Snowdonia. Also in sight are all the various obstacles including walls, trees, out-of-bounds, bunkers and hedgerows. The 2nd with its fairway on a slight incline features a ditch crossing the fairway and a well-positioned pond to the right some 126 yards from the green. Running parallel, the 3rd is slightly downhill and a well-struck drive settles into the neck of the narrowing fairway leaving a pitch shot to the longest green on the course with its slight hint of a Mackenzie surface.

Each hole at Caernarfon has its own Welsh name and *Y Dder-*

of the green appears to foreshorten the hole. It is important to believe the card's yardage and think distance to this tricky sloping green.

Hole 14, if my memory serves me well, has only in the last couple of years introduced out-of-bounds to the right of this short yet subtle dog-leg par-4. Of course it makes sense to play an iron off the tee in the direction of the straits beyond the downhill fairway, and then still be left with only a gentle pitch to the smallest green on the course. The over ambitious, using a wood, can so easily run out of fairway and into the hedge bordering the perimeter of the course.

The 15th, running parallel with Caernarfon Bay, is a gradual climb until about 50 yards short of the green. A completely blind second shot needs to be carried up the right side of the fairway due to the fact that once beyond the marker post the fairway does not just plunge down towards the green but also slopes sharply from right to left.

On the morning of my visit the last of the short holes played far beyond its card distance because of a strong north-easterly wind. It pays to play boldly to this bulbous shaped green with its narrow entrance. And so to the last – and longest – hole on the course. *Bryn Glas* (Green Hill) has few challenges in its early stages but it does become more demanding. A narrowing fairway has to its right a fairly recently constructed pond with two of the quietest and best behaved duck I have ever seen! The raised and well-designed stepped green could quite easily be the deciding factor in determining the winner or loser in any club competition.

*(PL)*

## Card of the course:

| | | | | | |
|---|---|---|---|---|---|
| 1. | 343 yards | par 4 | 10. | 210 yards | par 3 |
| 2. | 295 | 4 | 11. | 428 | 4 |
| 3. | 313 | 4 | 12. | 171 | 3 |
| 4. | 360 | 4 | 13. | 394 | 4 |
| 5. | 170 | 3 | 14. | 335 | 4 |
| 6. | 425 | 4 | 15. | 354 | 4 |
| 7. | 374 | 4 | 16. | 395 | 4 |
| 8. | 199 | 3 | 17. | 157 | 3 |
| 9. | 474 | 5 | 18. | 494 | 5 |
| Out: | 2953 yards | par 35 | | | |
| In: | 2938 yards | par 34 | | | |
| Total: | 5891 yards | par 69 | | s.s.s. 68 | |

# Caerwys (Nine of Clubs)

*3080 yards; par 60*

On the western edge of the pretty village of Caerwys can be found a unique golf course: it boasts a par-4 of only 165 yards! To be honest it is an eccentric hole, if fun, but it would be a pity to dismiss the course on the strength of this one extraordinary hole.

To do so would be to miss out on a number of short, but testing, genuine golf holes in lovely surroundings. The fairways are lush, the bunkers broad and deep, and the greens wickedly sloping but true. In fact I should say it would take the skills of an accomplished

**Caerwys 3rd**

golfer to score well here, despite the short length which might lead those accomplished golfers to assume this was only for beginners. Try it and see if I am right!

After a simple opening hole, the 2nd asks you to clear a cross-bunker but stop on the green which leans downhill from you. It is probably within the compass of the exhibition golfer to play a trick shot round the trees to find the 3rd green, but few others could aspire to control such a huge hook and going over the top of the trees is not an option. So a wedge is played out into the open space on the right and another wedge in through a gap in the bushes to a triple-decker green.

The 4th, too, can probably be driven, but again a long draw will have to be controlled. A straight drive is likely to find the 5th fairway and the pitch from there is simple enough, but do not try it when the course is crowded! The view down the valley from here is glorious.

For some reason the 5th, too, is rated as a par-4 but as even I can reach the green (albeit over the trees) with a 5-iron on the direct route this strikes me as being ultra-conservative. Three bunkers out on the right have to be avoided by those who choose to play the hole as a bogey-4. On both the 6th and 7th there is trouble on the left and the 8th is a real tester. Either you are on the green putting for two or you are reaching in your bag for another ball, with trees either side and dreadful trouble down to your left. The round ends with a gentle par-3 over a ridge, well-bunkered.

*(MR)*

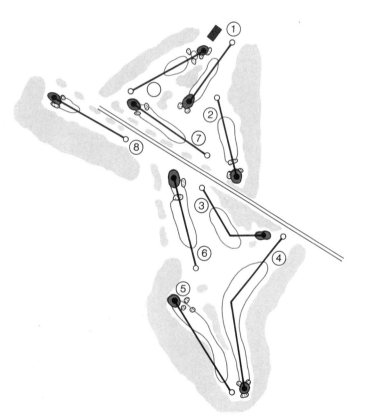

### Card of the course:

| | | |
|---|---|---|
| 1. | 137 yards | par 3 |
| 2. | 148 | 3 |
| 3. | 165 | 4 |
| 4. | 301 | 4 |
| 5. | 185 | 4 |
| 6. | 164 | 3 |
| 7. | 167 | 3 |
| 8. | 147 | 3 |
| 9. | 126 | 3 |
| Out: | 1540 yards | par 30 |
| Total: | 3080 yards | par 60 |

# *Chirk*

*7045 yards; par 72; s.s.s. 73*

Chirk Castle, it is said, is the only castle in the Marches to have been occupied continuously since it was built in the reign of Edward I. It superseded a smaller Norman structure a couple of miles away and in its turn was altered and added to as military needs gave way to more graceful living and now the forbidding towers and dungeons of the mediaeval castle contrast sharply with the luxurious staterooms in the Adam style. Magnificent formal gardens and a superb pair of wrought iron gates from 1721 complete the picture. This is canal country, too, with some of the most famous aqueducts in the land, and some of the least spoiled upland in Wales close at hand. Given the recent improvements in the roads around Chirk few will tarry long here preferring to speed to the more spectacular heights of Snowdonia or the beaches beyond. Golfers, however, might profitably interrupt their journey long enough to play one of the longest courses in Wales and, arguably, the longest hole in the country.

But Chirk is not to be played simply to collect statistics for no sooner have you put in print that here is the longest hole than someone comes along and builds one even longer. No, Chirk is to be played as a genuine test of technique and resolve and Roger Jones Consultants who built it will certainly keep you thinking throughout the round. Nor is the white course here reserved only for occasional exhibition matches. I played it with three members who habitually play the full course even for purely social golf and with four of the first five holes playing directly into a really stiff wind funnelled between the hills on either side it was quickly apparent just how long the course is.

In theory the 1st hole is a pushover, only 374 yards from the very back, but a ditch 200 yards out is at exactly the length most of our best drives return to earth. With a ridge before the green approach shots are difficult to judge. Into the full force of the wind the 2nd played as long as two wooden shots, and then the difficulty of crossing the ditch and avoiding the stream close at hand on the

right was made the more apparent. In such a wind the 3rd was a mere mid-iron but it still had to clear a ditch yet stop quickly on the other side. Trees constrict the entrance and bunkers eat into the sides of an already narrow green.

Now comes the first of three very substantial par-5s, and it is from the par-5s rather than the par-4s that Chirk gets most of its great length. The 4th is not too punishing and as long as the second shot clears a row of mounds in the fairway there should not be too many difficulties avoiding the several bunkers littering the fairway over the final 100 yards to a characteristically raised green. Taking us to the end of the course, the 5th is a dog-leg to the right past a mound and bunker. The green itself is high on a hillside above further bunkers, built on two levels, and by now it is becoming obvious that none of these greens is straightforward.

Certainly the next green, the 6th, is laid to USGA specifications implying that it can be made to putt very fast. The tee looks out from high ground onto a fairway curving right to left past a bunker. If you have the strength you might just clear that bunker. Otherwise you need to make allowance for the hill while selecting the best club to approach this rolling green. The 7th is similar, except that this time it is an out-of-bounds fence on the left with which you must flirt if you are to avoid being bundled off too far to the right by the sloping fairway. The green-side bunkering is notably tight.

Relief of a kind is available on the short 8th, but there are mounds and bunkers to punish on all sides. Leave the green by the back left and you stand on the tee of what is currently reckoned to be the longest hole in Great Britain. From whatever tee you play the hole it is a vigorous challenge and driving downhill the main object is avoiding the ditch and pond on the left. While there is plenty of room to the right the further you play safe the more you are making difficulties for yourself in trying to clear a ditch 150 yards in front of the green. Even a relatively short pitch shot is given a test in the elevation of the green and the positioning of its attendant bunkers. This is another green laid to USGA specifications. Apparently we have covered more than 3,500 yards without a par-4 of over 400 yards. Dispute the figures if you like, but in a near tempest all the par-4s seemed *far* longer!

Into the said wind, as often the 10th hole must play, most drives will land short of the ditch which crosses the fairway about 210 yards from the back tee. Will they run on into it? Can they be persuaded to clear it? If you opt to lay up short of the ditch you will have precious little chance of making the green at least 240 yards away with your next shot. Continuing in this direction the 11th may well be into the wind as well, distance being at a premium to grant a lofted iron approach over a leaning shoulder of land to a waisted green.

The 12th is simple enough: aim for the left front of the green and watch as the ball curls round wickedly to the right as it rolls across the hugely canted putting surface. There are no marks for

falling short on the direct line with the worst of four bunkers in wait. And yet another apparently short par-4 follows, the 13th, but as it plays directly into the south-west wind it seems somewhat longer. A really good drive passes between hidden bunkers yet avoids tangling with a mound on the left, the fairway tending to throw the ball that way. Then it is up over cavernous bunkers to a domed plateau green beyond which the 14th tee looks out on its relatively accessible green below. Then, played as a genuine par-5, the 15th is not too vicious but those with birdie aspirations will need to cheat the trees and a bunker on the left as they try to cut the corner of the fairway dog-leg.

Advantage, it is to be hoped, was taken of these few moments of respite for the final three holes demand quality play. There is nothing to hinder a good drive on the 16th but full use must be made of that for access to the green is on the far side of a stream and that same stream runs down the left side of the putting surface

*Chirk 9th*

while a deep bunker at the front narrows the entrance still further. Given also the borrows on the green and its narrow dumb-bell shape and it is quite clear why this hole is Stroke 2.

Still at full stretch we essay the 17th, again with nothing to hinder length on the drive but there is a ditch on the right waiting for the slightest push or fade. Blindly we blast away with our second shots in the general direction of the green. We have taken note of the ditch crossing the fairway but in all probability we will perish in the rough allowed to grow in between the ditch and a broad cross-bunker on the direct line. Avoid all these and you still need to keep clear of a long bunker hidden behind a mound on the left of the green.

To finish you are asked, once again, to decide whether or not you can clear a stream 225 yards out (implying, I suppose, a clean carry of the order of 240 yards). You know you cannot possibly do it, but the wind is at your back and you would not be seen dead with a 3-iron in your hand! Whether you go for the carry or not you will still be tested in finding the correct part of this rolling green almost 50 yards long.

Chirk is new and I am an old fashioned traditionalist but I am happy to concede that here the architecture is bold, the strategy always clear from the tee and the challenge considerable. With autumn leaves already golden on the surrounding hillsides I can wait for the multitudinous plantings of saplings to become trees.

*(MR)*

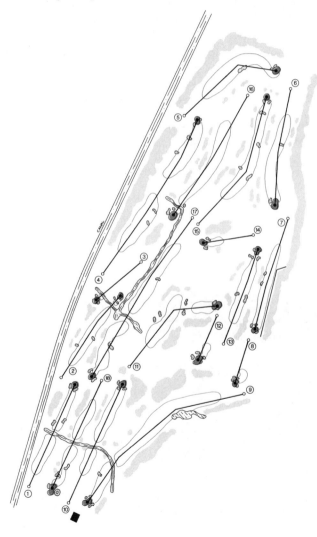

### Card of the course:

| 1. | 374 yards | par 4 | 10. | 439 yards | par 4 |
|---|---|---|---|---|---|
| 2. | 359 | 4 | 11. | 387 | 4 |
| 3. | 203 | 3 | 12. | 170 | 3 |
| 4. | 597 | 5 | 13. | 341 | 4 |
| 5. | 387 | 4 | 14. | 171 | 3 |
| 6. | 395 | 4 | 15. | 510 | 5 |
| 7. | 396 | 4 | 16. | 460 | 4 |
| 8. | 160 | 3 | 17. | 632 | 5 |
| 9. | 659 | 5 | 18. | 405 | 4 |

| Out: | 3530 yards | par 36 | | |
|---|---|---|---|---|
| In: | 3515 yards | par 36 | | |
| Total: | 7045 yards | par 72 | | s.s.s. 73 |

# Clays Farm

*5624 yards; par 69; s.s.s. 67*

**J**ust off the Wrexham-Holt road, a mere stone's throw from Wrexham Golf Club (or should it be a metaphorical *niblick*?), is Clays Farm, recently added to the limited roster of full 18-hole courses in this corner of North Wales. It is precisely the sort of course of which a great many are needed throughout the kingdom: a properly constructed course at a green fee most can afford, simple in strategy so that those who are less gifted are not seriously hindered from making forward progress yet serious enough to give a decent game to the more proficient. There are no forced carries over acres of gorse or quarries; there are no blind shots in regulation play; there are few obstacles within the fairways themselves; the greens are thoughtfully contoured though sparingly bunkered; and there is a driving range, so no one has an excuse for duffing the first tee shot! I am sure a course of this nature is far more encouraging to the aspirant golfer than some of the tricked up par-3 and executive courses which require considerable pitching and chipping skills if ever one is to get the ball to stop on their tiny, wildly sloping greens.

The first three holes should get play flowing well with only a hedge on the left to be avoided. The 4th is a right-hand dog-leg which will become tighter as the young trees, around which the fairway bends, grow taller and stouter. Tree planting at Clays Farm has been generous, but it is a mature specimen to the right of the 5th green into which many a sliced tee shot will clatter. I suspect sliced tee shots may abound also on the 6th and 7th as the fairways of both are narrow and bounded to the left by out-of-bounds hedges. The 7th is a tough hole by any standards, the fairway curving left along the hedge, the second shot having to be squeezed

*Clays Farm 11th*

through the narrow gap between the hedge and a wood to find a raised green with boggy ground below on the right.

The 8th and 9th should allow us to consolidate before the 10th winds uphill to the right past a tree and the remains of a hedge left to grow where so many of us will mis-hit our second shots. (The obvious route, up the 11th fairway, is out-of-bounds.) I wonder how long the 11th will retain its lowly stroke rating of 17, for it looks to have the makings of one of those roguish short par-4s

which are terribly simple most of the time but on which a cricket score is easily run up if you tangle with the hedge, trees or ditch just off the green on the left? The 12th and 13th are straightforward enough, and so is the drive on the 14th, but here the pitch is not quite so simple, being slightly downhill over bunkers.

In an effort to avoid the hedge on the left of the 15th around which the fairway bends many will make the hole much longer for themselves, while birdie hunters will have to chance their arm with the out-of-bounds. Longer hitters will need to avoid driving into the pond which cuts across the 16th fairway, and for most of us the best policy will be to try to place the tee shot where we are left with a full shot with a short iron in to the green rather than risk fluffing a half-hit wedge.

Few golfers of my sort will drive the 17th green with the threat of out-of-bounds omnipresent on the left and the need to carry the ball up the rise onto the putting surface. We will all want to try to cut the corner on the 18th and the penalty for failure is plainly visible from the tee!

*(MR)*

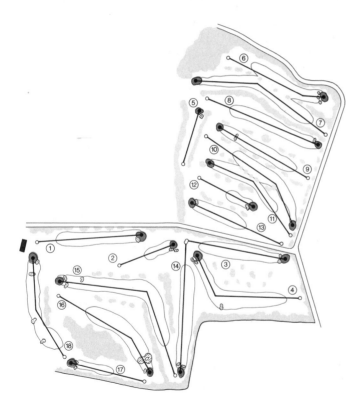

| Card of the course: | | | | | |
|---|---|---|---|---|---|
| 1. | 301 yards | par 4 | 10. | 382 yards | par 4 |
| 2. | 170 | 3 | 11. | 335 | 4 |
| 3. | 346 | 4 | 12. | 183 | 3 |
| 4. | 373 | 4 | 13. | 284 | 4 |
| 5. | 138 | 3 | 14. | 367 | 4 |
| 6. | 310 | 4 | 15. | 510 | 5 |
| 7. | 430 | 4 | 16. | 358 | 4 |
| 8. | 352 | 4 | 17. | 222 | 3 |
| 9. | 303 | 4 | 18. | 260 | 4 |
| Out: | 2723 yards | par 34 | | | |
| In: | 2901 yards | par 35 | | | |
| Total: | 5624 yards | par 69 | | s.s.s. 67 | |

# Conwy

*6647 yards; par 72; s.s.s. 72*

In the late 1970s it seemed to many Conwy members that civilisation was about to end. The improvements to the A55 North Wales Coast Road threatened to remove one of the loveliest stretches of golf in existence, that part of Conwy's back nine that rambled through the densest of gorse bushes in utter seclusion at the end of a round which had begun with a drive down a lane, over a cattle grid, and past the salt marshes. But the club and course had survived many previous disasters in their long history and a virtue would be made out of necessity. (Those disasters had included military occupation in both World Wars – a good part of Mulberry Harbour being constructed just behind what is now the 2nd green – and a club house fire in 1933).

Nor was the course unused to change. Back in 1876 a number of members of the Royal Liverpool Club brought Jack Morris, the club's professional, brother of the famous Tom Morris of St. Andrews, to the Morfa, that flat protrusion of natural linksland at the mouth of the River Conwy. Realising the potential of this ideal golfing land Morris laid out a 9-hole course which remained for five years. Then in 1890 the club was properly organised and a new 9-hole course laid out thus becoming established as the third oldest golf club in Wales. (Tenby Golf Club, the oldest, had been formed some nineteen months earlier). Five years later a full 18-hole course was again the brain child of the Royal Liverpool Club's professional and by 1896 the popularity of the game was such that an item appeared in the suggestion book, reading, "There are 150-odd members in the club and only five large tumblers. I suggest that more be provided."

The course did not remain static thereafter, alterations of one sort or another evolving fairly naturally until, about a century after the very first golf was played here, Frank Pennink was commissioned to make substantial changes to those holes furthest from the clubhouse. These were further refined in 1983 by the highly respected professionals, Brian Huggett and Neil Coles, alongside their more sweeping changes to the back nine necessitated by construction of the Conwy Tunnel and A55 Expressway. A course of just short of 7,000 yards from the very back blue Championship tees resulted, maintaining its position as one of the top two or three courses in the north of the Province, a position reinforced by its continued hosting of genuine championship events.

Conwy has been host to numerous Welsh Amateur Championships since 1899, the Welsh Stroke Play and umpteen junior championships. The Welsh Ladies have contested their Championship here many times and both the British Ladies Amateur Championship and their Stroke Play came to Conwy in the 1980s, the latter returning in 1996. Add to them the World One Arm Championships (an outstanding event in 1990), the European Boys' Team Championships in 1992 and, perhaps the greatest honour, the Home Internationals in 1990. On the professional front 1966 saw Conwy as the hosts of the Welsh PGA Championships and in 1970 the Martini International Tournament was held there. Regrettably it gained little publicity because of a press strike, but still the crowds flocked to see such stars as Bobby Locke, Peter Alliss and the late, big-hitting Harry Weetman. A score of 268 saw joint winners, Peter Thomson of Australia and Doug Sewell of Ferndown sharing the spoils.

As the club's Professional for the last three decades I feel proud to have followed such well-known men as Fred Bullock, runner-up to Gary Player in the 1959 Open Championship; also the Open Champion of 1920 and Ryder Cup Captain, George Duncan, of whom it was said that he went up to the top of Conwy Mountain, teed his ball on the face of his gold watch and drove it straight over the railway lines onto the Morfa. So let us return to the Morfa and golf.

The opening hole with out-of-bounds some 40 yards right of the generously wide fairway would appear relatively straightforward except for a ridge and a downhill apron to the front of the green which can send the ball scuttling away through the back leaving a difficult downhill chip shot. Rather as at Troon the first time visitor (the long-standing member too, for that matter) may be lulled into a false sense of security. There are none of the towering sand dunes of Birkdale or Ballybunion, the greens seem flattish for the most part and fairway bunkering is sparing at least over the early holes. But it is rare for there to be no wind and very frequently it bludgeons in from the west round the headland making life very difficult on the 3rd, 5th, 11th, 12th, 13th and 17th in particular. At other times it whistles up the Conwy Valley making

those holes easier and their opposite numbers correspondingly tough. Hardly ever do consecutive holes run in the same direction and so at all times players must adapt their games and strategies to cope, even on the putting green.

The first of the par-3s (and in my opinion the best) can be a real teaser so early in the round with, again, out-of-bounds to the right and five guardian bunkers. It is played from a slightly elevated tee to a two-tier green surrounded by hummocks. Nor is leniency shown on the 3rd hole, although not overlong in yardage for a par-4, with, yet again, out-of-bounds plus the beach on the right

*Conwy 17th*

and, invariably, a south-westerly to contend with when playing the approach shot to the green, very exposed up on its plateau above the estuary. Downwind a big drive easily reaches the foot of the green but it can be the devil's own job trying to stop even the shortest of pitches on it.

Tee up with care on the 4th as the 10th fairway runs adjacent. This dog-leg to the left which was redesigned several years ago requires careful assessment on the second shot to the green as a ridge some 90 yards short of the target tends to make the green appear closer than it is. Only three bunkers play their part on this hole: two to the right of the fairway which can catch the slightest pushed tee shot and just one beside the green into which almost all feeble approaches are drawn.

With its white and blue tees secreted away in the gorse bushes the 5th is one of those holes on which one can be gripped by the teeth of the so often strong prevailing wind. With its relatively bare and sandy-based fairway anything but the purest of strikes can lead to trouble with gorse bushes on the right, and bunkers short of the green both left and right. The following short hole has its teeing area situated amidst more gorse and runs parallel with the sand dunes. Although it would appear a straightforward par-3 one must not be complacent. Indeed, it would be a nondescript hole on an inland, parkland course, but with no trees to aid distance judgement it is a classic seaside hole.

The 7th is played from an elevated tee with only sand dunes dividing it from the sea, and what a tee it is! However mediocre the preceding golf, it would be an insensitive human whose spirits were not raised by the maritime vista on the left. There is golfing treachery down that side in the form of thick rough, rock roses, humps and hollows, but by playing the hole in an orthodox manner there are rewards to be had in the gathering, bottle-neck shaped approach to a low-lying, sheltered green, whose slopes are not the easiest to read.

Conwy has a gem of a setting and the views can be savoured from no finer a point than the 8th tee with the boats wending their way up and down the estuary, Llandudno's Great Orme in the distance on the far side, Puffin Island several miles out to sea and Anglesey beyond it. The backcloth to the hole is Conwy Mountain with its colours changing not only with the seasons but also the time of day. I can clearly remember one day back in the late '60s when I was golfing with the club's Vice-President, Tommy "Tubby" Owen, a much travelled man, who told me that I would

have to travel a long way to find a finer view anywhere in the world, the equal of Pebble Beach or Cypress Point. Turn your gaze to the left and beyond the marina you might pick out Conwy's historic bridges leading to the little town now so much more attractive that the tunnel has taken away the unbearable congestion and incessant flow of articulated lorries lumbering through the old town walls and past the majestic castle dating back to the reign of Edward I in 1287. Returning to the golf, a wide open fairway with little trouble awaits on the 8th. A mean strike will see your ball well over the road followed by a long iron to a two-tier green with only a solitary bunker on the left short of the green. Into the wind, however, this already lengthy hole becomes quite awesome.

As I said earlier, fairway bunkers are few on these links, although the 9th is an exception. This slight dog-leg with internal out-of-bounds to its left displays a trio of them positioned approximately 90 yards short of the putting surface. Course management is the order of the day here. The prodigious hitter sees it as a birdiable hole and invariably sets his sights on being up in two shots, that is providing the hummocks just short of the green are carried. Lesser mortals are happy coming away with a par having played short of the bunkers on the second shot and successfully negotiated the highest part of the hill which cuts off the green from the right-hand side of the fairway. 35 shots (with handicap, of course!) is hardly an ungenerous allowance for the front nine.

The back nine however, with a score more bunkers, is a true test of character. The 10th with its undulating fairway, half a dozen traps and a smattering of gorse is just a hint of things to come, but the 11th hole, with one of the very few long carries to the fairway, has a glut of bushes to negotiate from the tee, and is a devil of an alternative starting point. Depending on the elements it can play very long to a well-guarded green. As with the 11th, the 12th also falls foul of the wind. I have so often seen golfers with heads down and backs stooped battling up what seems a never ending hole. Bushes and bunkers again can be a great spoiler half way down the fairway. For the average hitter the hole plays as a genuine par-5.

Still into the wind and in the heart of the sand dunes the 13th demands thoughtful club selection with a good deal depending on which level of the Mackenzie green the hole has been cut. There is a little open ground to bale out on the right but there can be terrible trouble amongst the gorse and bramble bushes, cavernous bunkers and tumbling hollows on the left. Standing above all this on the elevated 14th tee with the wind behind there is great

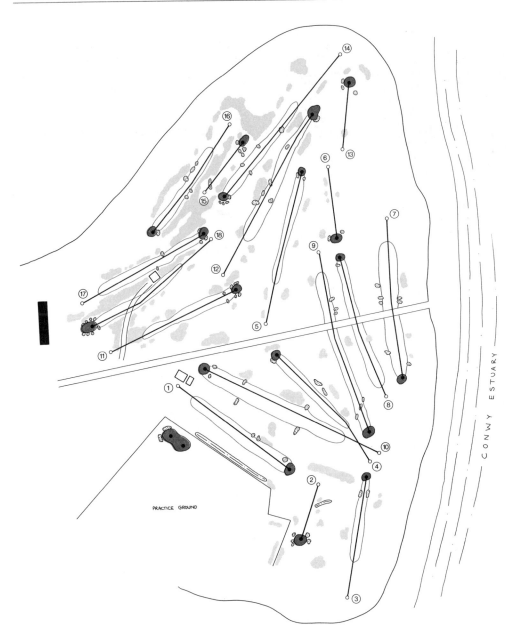

PRACTICE GROUND

CONWY ESTUARY

temptation to open the shoulders. Do so with caution as the Morfa's natural hazards begin to close in (though some of the denser patches of gorse have been thinned out in recent years not only to regenerate the remaining bushes but also to speed up play for visiting parties). Neither should you be fooled by the ridge 100 yards from the target which tends to make the hole appear shorter. Playing one club stronger will do no harm.

The last of the short holes comes next with the teeing ground tucked away among yet more gorse bushes. Correct club selection is vital (and tricky as the shelter afforded by the gorse bushes tends to obscure the full effect of the wind), four bunkers lying in wait for anyone who underclubs, while overclubbing will see your ball disappear into the deepest of gorse to be followed by a discussion on the rules of golf in deciding where and how to drop out!

Conwy has its own *Amen Corner*. The first of these has just been played and the final three holes constitute the remainder. The rich blaze of yellow which envelopes the 16th fairway can be a daunting sight. A cool head or a calm nerve is required to play this slight dog-leg in par or better, particularly from the championship tee far back amidst the bushes. Even from the front tee perfect line is needed not to perish in the jungle on the right or the bunkers recently introduced on the left.

The 17th is a notorious card wrecker, as infamous in this part of Wales as the *Road Hole* at St. Andrews or the *Railway Hole* at Troon, with the narrowest of fairways threaded through impenetrable gorse on both sides made all the more daunting by the angle at which the tee is set. The gorse runs the entire length of the hole on the left and almost as far on the right preying on the mind on every shot. An iron off the tee may seem prudent but in any sort of wind (and this hole often plays directly into the full force of the wind) that leaves an extremely demanding second shot to the well-bunkered green. If one has the courage and skill to thread a wood shot down this alley one can be left with a somewhat easier approach. But what courage and skill it takes!

The 18th hole can also bring tears to the eyes of the man who thinks he has the monthly medal sewn up. The recommended line from the tee is the club's flagpole. Any ball hit only slightly right can often end up in the bushes and while many who are nursing a good score will opt for the apparent safety on the left they may find their second shot dreadfully perilous played blind across a huge bank of gorse bushes all carry with a longish iron. A steep ridge across the fairway tells us we are 150 yards from the heart of the green, but yet again the right-hand side of the green is flanked with gorse bushes and four bunkers and there is similar on the left.

Interestingly this is one of the greens closest to the clubhouse and marina which has changed contours in recent years. An extract from the suggestion book of 1896 reads, "That shoes should be obtained for the horse or other animal used in rolling the greens; horses' hoofs cut up the greens shockingly as they pulled the roller today." A century later those greens are some of the truest to be found as several players in the Home Internationals testified. Now the home green is overlooked by a brand new and very comfortable two-storey clubhouse in best "towers and turrets" style with far-reaching panoramic views, a far cry from a century ago when Conwy's first club house was the front room of Miss Walker's boarding house.

Perhaps the Greens Committee caught a glimpse of my draft article! Since I wrote it, they have added a number of fairway bunkers over the front nine, significantly tightening the 1st, 4th and 8th drives.

*(PL)*

| Card of the Course: | | | | | |
|---|---|---|---|---|---|
| 1. | 375 yards | par 4 | 10. | 537 yards | par 5 |
| 2. | 147 | 3 | 11. | 385 | 4 |
| 3. | 335 | 4 | 12. | 503 | 5 |
| 4. | 393 | 4 | 13. | 174 | 3 |
| 5. | 442 | 4 | 14. | 499 | 5 |
| 6. | 177 | 3 | 15. | 153 | 3 |
| 7. | 441 | 4 | 16. | 363 | 4 |
| 8. | 435 | 4 | 17. | 389 | 4 |
| 9. | 523 | 5 | 18. | 376 | 4 |
| Out: | 3268 yards | par 35 | | | |
| In: | 3379 yards | par 37 | | | |
| Total: | 6647 yards | par 72 | | s.s.s. 72 | |

# Criccieth

*5787 yards; par 69; s.s.s. 68*

Criccieth's roots as a Victorian seaside resort are evident in its architecture. It is a picturesque, unassuming little town with two excellent sandy beaches which are separated by a prominent headland crowned by the ruined walls and ragged towers of Criccieth Castle. The approach to the golf course involves an uphill climb of about two miles from the heart of the town and the terrain changes rapidly to a gently rolling moorland. Following a public meeting the club was founded in 1905 and the chairman of the

**Criccieth 2nd/18th**

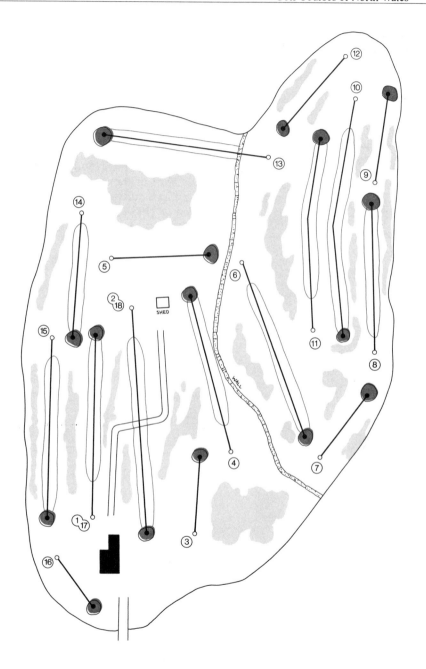

steering committee was William George, the brother of David George, later to become known better-known as David *Lloyd* George. It might come as a surprise to learn that he was actually born in Manchester!

The 18-hole links, as it was referred to at that time, was laid out by a Mr. A. Matthews from Rhyl for a fee of £200. Tom Morris laid out the Royal County Down links in 1889 for a sum not exceeding £4. The fees commanded by Nicklaus, Trent Jones, Dye and Palmer can run into millions. Golf course architecture is like fine wine: there are bargains and, equally, you can jolly well pay for what you get.....In the early 1950s the course was reduced to 9-holes and so it remained until in the early '70s it became a unique 16-hole course, and in order to make up the full round the golfer plays the 1st and 2nd as holes 17 and 18. I am given to understand that there are plans afoot to create new 17th and 18th holes.

The 1st of the current 16 holes, with its recently introduced out-of-bounds both right and left of the fairway, is not, however, over-taxing (as can be said of several holes on this course). The next hole has a blind second shot as the fairway swoops down to a low-lying green. I found the positioning of the 3rd tee rather perplexing as it sits high up on a hillock some distance from the 2nd green.

Moving on a little, the 6th, a splendid par-4 with a lengthy carry from the tee over rough and marram grass, does not go without its problems round the green with a spinney and rough ground in proximity. The 10th is an interesting, downhill dog-leg par-5 with an eye-catching symmetrical row of trees which stands to the side and back of the green. Emphasis is on a long and accurate tee shot at the uphill 11th in order to get a clear view of the green for your second shot.

As I walked around the course I had pangs of nostalgia for my days as a young Assistant Professional at Davyhulme Park and my early years at Conwy on seeing greens mown by hand as in bygone times. Although somewhat time-consuming to achieve, a finer cut is hard to find. Nearing the end of the round, the 15th is certainly a hole to be reckoned with, a stone wall bounding the right side from tee to green. Having negotiated the tee shot successfully the challenge really starts with rocky outcrops and boulders at the foot of the huge hill and a run up of some 50 yards to a pulpit green, and woe betide should you be left with a downhill putt from the back of the green!

The last hole has, I am sure, proven most irritating to many a golfer. O how difficult to judge from the heights of the tee the low-lying square green! There is a golden rule – don't overshoot the putting surface as the results could be catastrophic.

*(PL)*

### Card of the course:

| | | | | | |
|---|---|---|---|---|---|
| 1. | 383 yards | par 4 | 10. | 489 yards | par 5 |
| 2. | 500 | 5 | 11. | 404 | 4 |
| 3. | 165 | 3 | 12. | 219 | 3 |
| 4. | 338 | 4 | 13. | 358 | 4 |
| 5. | 223 | 3 | 14. | 262 | 4 |
| 6. | 410 | 4 | 15. | 373 | 4 |
| 7. | 164 | 3 | 16. | 113 | 3 |
| 8. | 323 | 4 | 17. | 383 | 4 |
| 9. | 180 | 3 | 18. | 500 | 5 |

| | | | | |
|---|---|---|---|---|
| Out: | 2686 yards | par 33 | | |
| In: | 3101 yards | par 36 | | |
| Total: | 5787 yards | par 69 | s.s.s. 68 | |

# Denbigh

*5712 yards; par 69; s.s.s. 68*

It is good to see Denbigh restored to the status of a county. It has an engaging county town, complete with ruined castle, market cross, Town Hall and thatched cockpit. In 1928 it cost 2d. to travel by bus from Denbigh to the golf course, which had been revived in 1922. Then it was a 9-hole course, laid out by John Stockton, the first club professional. Land came and went, but it was not until 1986 that Craig Defoy opened the 18-hole course we know today.

As the football commentator said of the match, "It is a game of two halves", and so it now is at Denbigh with a complete change in character from the exposed heathland roaming the hill behind

**Denbigh 1st**

the clubhouse to rolling parkland on the far side of the B5382. These parkland holes are the more recent, but you would hardly guess, so grand and noble are the venerable trees which oversee play on this section of the course. It would imply tedium (which is far from the case) to suggest that the holes on this half are identical, but it is true to say that each sweeps down before sweeping up, the trees tending to restrict options on the second shot, with the result that it will be unusual if the golfer has not had to improvise at least one shot over or under the branches before crossing the road to the 8th. As someone who is spiritually more at home amidst the dunes of the seaside links or the open spaces of the blasted heath I am more than ready to acknowledge my immediate attraction to these parkland holes at Denbigh.

As early as the 1st tee the nature of the task is made apparent. On a straight hole of no great length the necessity is to place the drive in such a spot that there is some hope of finding the rolling green with the second shot. The golf heads for the open country on the 2nd, but not before you have driven down an avenue of trees towards the marker post from which the fairway bears right over artful ridges to the green. This is the longest of the par-4s and most golfers will find most of the par-4s here in range of two shots, but only if they have chosen the best line from the tee. Even the gentle 3rd is governed by those trees around which this part of the course was so cunningly laid out.

Only on the 4th is the first sand-trap of the round encountered, awaiting those who approach the green too fearful of the hedge close on the left of the green. There is another on the right of the 5th green, but it is only one of several serious lines of defence, the fairway turning sharply to the left and uphill as trees pinch the fairway on the approach. This hole is strong enough to be rated 1st Stroke Hole. The 6th and 7th take play out to the west and back before a

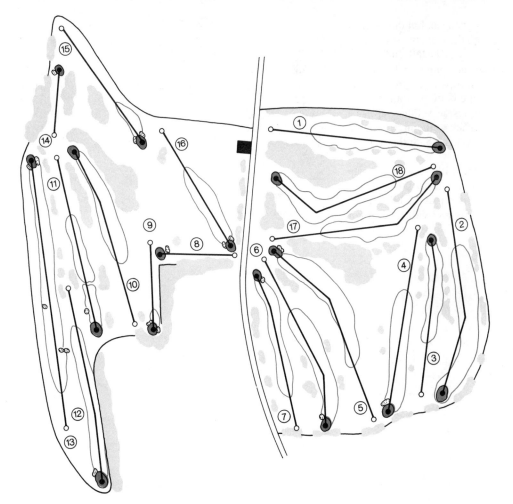

pair of short holes closes this part of the round.

It is a feature of two of the greatest golf courses on earth (Cypress Point and Ballybunion) that par-3 holes follow back-to-back. Denbigh goes even better by having *two* pairs of such holes. The 8th is more a matter of club selection, climbing over a cross-bunker and past a tree, but the 9th is splendid, dropping gently through rocks and gorse to a green framed by trees beyond which the Clwydian Hills lead the eye past Dyserth Mountain to the distant sea at Prestatyn and Rhyl.

Up here the character of the land has changed, but though this is more in the nature of windswept upland there are trees to define the drive on the 10th as it curves deliberately to the left. Judgement of the pitch, running downhill, is the essence of the 11th, and the 12th completes the descent, the drive needing to avoid trees on the left to find the centre of the fairway at the bottom of a dip from which the pitch is up to a ledge green alongside a stone wall. The only par-5, the 13th, is a lengthy climb back to the high ground, most of the trouble being on the left, towards which the fairway leans.

The second pair of par-3s follows, the 14th very short to an exposed green, the 15th a full wooden shot for most of us, bunkers on either side of the green. Though the drive may be blind from the 16th tee, in reality it is downhill and many will fancy their chances of putting for two. For the final two holes play reverts to the parkland over the road, parallel holes sweeping down and up, curving all the time and stern in the demands they make on perfect placing of the drive. These greens, like so many during the course of the round with their many slopes and borrows, can be ticklish to read.

*(MR)*

### Card of the course:

| No. | Yards | Par | No. | Yards | Par |
|---|---|---|---|---|---|
| 1. | 342 yards | par 4 | 10. | 327 yards | par 4 |
| 2. | 408 | 4 | 11. | 339 | 4 |
| 3. | 295 | 4 | 12. | 378 | 4 |
| 4. | 363 | 4 | 13. | 524 | 5 |
| 5. | 391 | 4 | 14. | 127 | 3 |
| 6. | 350 | 4 | 15. | 236 | 3 |
| 7. | 309 | 4 | 16. | 272 | 4 |
| 8. | 147 | 3 | 17. | 373 | 4 |
| 9. | 175 | 3 | 18. | 356 | 4 |
| Out: | 2780 yards | par 34 | | | |
| In: | 2932 yards | par 35 | | | |
| Total: | 5712 yards | par 69 | | s.s.s. 68 | |

# Dolgellau

*4671 yards; par 66; s.s.s. 63*

The striking, but small, town of Dolgellau lies in the long valley of the Mawddach River running inland from Barmouth under the long mountain spine of Cader Idris. Those who appreciate austere beauty find satisfaction in the grey architecture of this place which springs naturally from the geography of the cliff stone around it.

The bridge over the river here is one of the town's notable features, built in 1638 with seven arches which manage to be both graceful and strong, almost a golfing analogy. A mile or more out of the town centre lies the golf course, founded in 1911 on quite undulating yet fertile ground, giving a round which is not too strenuous

**Dolgellau 3rd**

yet contrasting with the links courses at nearby Aberdovey or Harlech.

The opening hole offers few problems, a good drive leaving a short pitch to a green which slopes deceptively from left to right. The 3rd hole, playing back towards the clubhouse is, however, demanding all the way. Only a good drive is rewarded with a clear sight of the green which must be approached from the right side of the sloping fairway. Then it is across the road, past the clubhouse, to the rest of the course. The 4th is routine, but the par-3 5th is not just a splendid hole in its own right. It offers from both tee and green inspiring views of Mynydd Moel and Cader Idris and beyond to the Mawddach estuary.

The par-4 6th is full of interest from the tee. Driving over a deep depression in the fairway is the first difficulty to be overcome, to which are added three cunningly positioned fairway bunkers readily placed to snaffle a shot only the slightest bit off centre. Then it is a blind, downhill second shot to the green which has three bunkers through the back waiting to punish the over-zealous approach. From the 7th tee the drive is played blind into a slight valley with a ditch which runs the full width of the fairway, creating various difficulties especially if the second shot misses the small, elevated green.

With just two holes to play, the next par-3 features a very sheer drop to a well-protected green. The final hole on this most scenic of 9-hole courses demands an accurate and powerful tee shot over an abundance of trouble which includes trees, gorse and scrubland. Although the course is short its uphill, downhill and side-hill lies make scoring quite challenging. Like so many 9-hole layouts in this book there are alternative tees to make the back-nine a little longer than the front.

*(PL)*

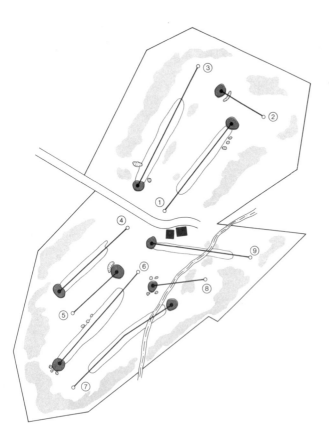

| Card of the course: | | | | | |
|---|---|---|---|---|---|
| 1. | 295 yards | par 4 | 10. | 295 yards | par 4 |
| 2. | 132 | 3 | 11. | 132 | 3 |
| 3. | 376 | 4 | 12. | 383 | 4 |
| 4. | 255 | 4 | 13. | 255 | 4 |
| 5. | 162 | 3 | 14. | 184 | 3 |
| 6. | 349 | 4 | 15. | 362 | 4 |
| 7. | 337 | 4 | 16. | 337 | 4 |
| 8. | 130 | 3 | 17. | 130 | 3 |
| 9. | 274 | 4 | 18. | 283 | 4 |
| Out: | 2310 yards | par 33 | | | |
| In: | 2361 yards | par 33 | | | |
| Total: | 4671 yards | par 66 | s.s.s. 63 | | |

# Ffestiniog

*5022 yards; par 68; s.s.s. 66*

The town of Ffestiniog is a neighbour of bigger and better-known Blaenau Ffestiniog and the 9-hole golf course is situated on rugged moorland some 1250 feet above sea level. The history of the club dates back to 1893 but, sadly, the original club folded in 1935. Happily, after great public demand, the course was reopened in 1967.

The 1st hole is a delightful par-3 named *Pont Sion* (John's Bridge). The green on the other side of the hollow sits several feet higher than the teeing ground. To the right of the green the ground falls away at a very acute angle: avoid this area at all costs! It can so easily be three off the 1st tee.

Tee No.2 faces Cardigan Bay. This par-4 known as *Gors Fawr*

*Ffestiniog 5th*

(The Big Marsh) can be approached by big hitters directly over the marsh leaving only the shortest of pitches, but there may well be negative thoughts in the minds of higher handicap players faced with the carry over the ooze. Good course management will tell them to play the dog-leg round the long way and beware of the

fairway sloping left to right: allow for that slice! *Giât Goch* (Red Gate) is the title given to the 3rd hole, again around 300 yards long. A stone wall marks the boundary of the course and a wayward shot will incur the out-of-bounds penalty.

A lake just 10 yards in front of the tee makes the 6th hole, *Llyn Ffridd* (Lake Ffridd), extremely intimidating. A carry of at least 150 yards is needed to clear the water. Having negotiated the drive safely there should be few problems on the rest of this short par-4. It is followed by another blind tee shot on the 7th, *Garreg Lwyd* (Grey Boulder). A clean strike will put you on to the right side of the slightly sloping left to right fairway. A perfect pitch is required for the tricky second shot to this dog-leg hole. A player who two putts this green should come away smiling and the person who one putts should buy the drinks (you will understand why!)

A demanding drive to an alley-wide fairway is necessary at the 9th, *Penffridd* (End of Mountain Pasture), and the glorious back-drop of the Moelwyn Mountains gives this a picture postcard setting. It is not surprising that a hole-in-one has never been recorded on any hole of this golf course. Perhaps some of the finest views in Wales are too distracting.

*(PL)*

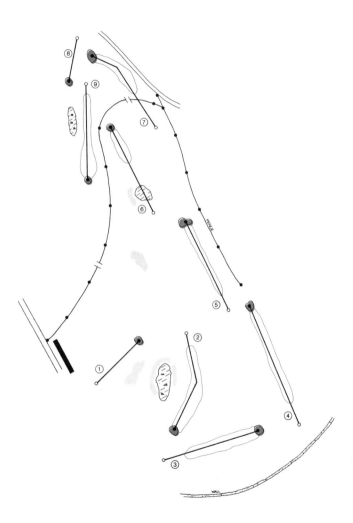

| Card of the course: | | | |
|---|---|---|---|
| 1. | 179 yards | par 3 | |
| 2. | 337 | 4 | |
| 3. | 312 | 4 | |
| 4. | 374 | 4 | |
| 5. | 279 | 4 | |
| 6. | 278 | 4 | |
| 7. | 334 | 4 | |
| 8. | 131 | 3 | |
| 9. | 287 | 4 | |
| Out: | 2511 yards | par 34 | |
| Total: | 5022 yards | par 68 | s.s.s. 66 |

# *Flint*

*5980 yards; par 70; s.s.s. 69*

**Flint 1st**

It is exhilarating – or awe inspiring depending on the reliability of your golf – to drink in the view from the 1st tee at Flint, the ledge green a very full shot away on the other side of a yawning ravine, majestic trees towering around you. The little town of Flint is hardly memorable, despite its unique castle, and you really have no idea what to expect as you set off up the back road that leads to the hospital, Cornist Park and the golf course. What you get for your (very modest) green fee is a lovely 9-hole course with fine views stretching from the hills at Helsby and Frodsham in Cheshire, over the Dee Estuary from Chester to Hoylake, and (in good weather) to the distinctive towers of the twin Cathedrals in Liverpool. Despite the views the golf course will demand your full attention for it is not one on which the prodigal will thrive. There are plans to expand to 18 holes soon. If the extra 9 are half as full of character as the existing layout this will be a cracker of a course.

If your nerve held and you found the 1st green you will suddenly realise that next time round this hole will be 30 yards longer and played from a tee just sufficiently to the right to accentuate even more the slopes around the green. The next hole is no easy matter, either, particularly when played from the 11th competition tee, far back in the trees. The drive has to be long to find the fairway which slopes down all the time to a stream on the left. It is safer on the high ground to the right but the hole is then made longer and the next shot will be played from a very side-hill lie. First timers should note that there is a new green some 30 yards beyond the original and the eye is easily deceived as to the real distance to the putting surface.

Until recently the 3rd was a long par-4 up an avenue of trees, so long and so uphill that few could hope to get home in two. It is now a par-5 but it is still long and still uphill and still up that same avenue of trees. It is not a difficult hole if you hit straight and firmly but, as on so many fairways here, the slopes frequently punish the slice or hook mercilessly.

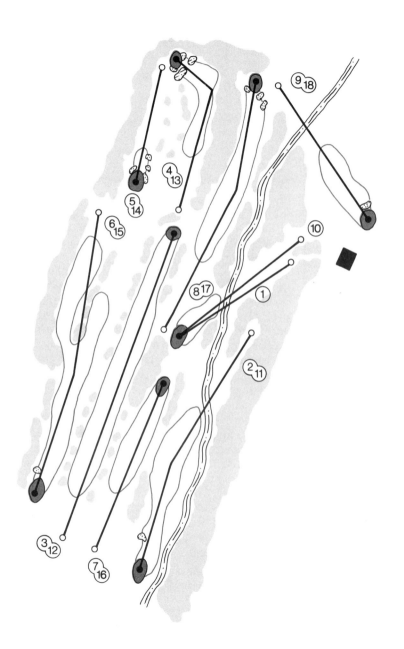

They used to say that you should drink a bottle of *Clos Vougeot* before buying it. It was a way of saying that it was such a variable wine, fabled though it was, that until you had enough experience of it you could not tell what you would be getting for your money. This absurd analogy came into my mind as I played the 4th – a hole you really should play several times before playing it for real. It is a short par-4 card wrecker the like of which I have come across only once before (at Dukinfield east of Manchester). The sensible take a 5-iron and keep it on the fairway a little to the right of the electricity pylon around which the hole bends. It is still only a short iron in from there. The mighty attempt the carry on the direct route but they must be aware that the intervening ground is out of bounds and that this green is amply guarded by two ponds and a pair of bunkers. The short hole which follows plays shorter than appearances suggest and offers panoramic views. The hedge to its right will force many a shot into the string of bunkers on the left.

Driving is stringently tested on the 6th with trees closing in from the left and houses cutting in on the right. There is no option other than booming a long, high drive out over the trees on the left and fading it slightly to get the maximum run down the fairway. Even when you have achieved that you are not home and dry with big slopes complicating the run in to the green, awful trouble on the right, trees on the left, and the green itself a ledge at the bottom of a slope. The 7th is gentler but not one on which suddenly to develop a slice!

The toughest hole on the course (but several run it close) is the 8th. The drive is uncompromising in the extreme with out-of-bounds on the left and a drop to perdition on the right. The fairway climbs inexorably and two shots will not see many golfers onto the green. The hedge which forms the boundary on the left curves and so does the fairway as it progresses so that from afar the green is inaccessible to many approaches, almost round the corner to the left. Happily, the final hole is a driveable par-4 across the ravine to the broadest of meadows.

And so you set off for the second circuit, undoubtedly wiser. After you have finished and enjoyed a pint or two you return to the locker room to collect your belongings. You notice a certain "coldness". It is the ghost of the Grey Lady. There is character aplenty on the course and not a little off it!

*(MR)*

### Card of the course:

| | | | | | | |
|---|---|---|---|---|---|---|
| 1. | 219 yards | par 3 | | 10. | 249 yards | par 3 |
| 2. | 403 | 4 | | 11. | 419 | 4 |
| 3. | 485 | 5 | | 12. | 504 | 5 |
| 4. | 273 | 4 | | 13. | 273 | 4 |
| 5. | 182 | 3 | | 14. | 179 | 3 |
| 6. | 450 | 4 | | 15. | 446 | 4 |
| 7. | 268 | 4 | | 16. | 285 | 4 |
| 8. | 423 | 4 | | 17. | 416 | 4 |
| 9. | 253 | 4 | | 18. | 253 | 4 |

| | | | |
|---|---|---|---|
| Out: | 2956 yards | par 35 | |
| In: | 3024 yards | par 35 | |
| Total: | 5980 yards | par 70 | s.s.s. 69 |

# Hawarden

*5894 yards; par 69; s.s.s. 68*

North Wales is littered with castles (this book, too, for that matter), most of them built by Edward I in his attempts to control the Welsh. As an Englishman writing a book about golf courses in North Wales I am obviously on dangerous political territory, but when he built his castle at Hawarden he was utilising the site of an Iron Age fort no less, the first bit of high ground on the Welsh side of Chester. They were not the Welsh but the Parliamentarians who demolished most of the castle and in time (around 1750) a more

**Hawarden 18th**

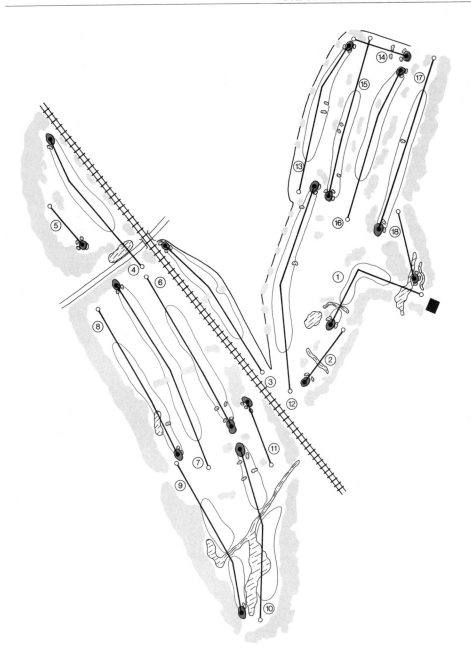

gracious residence was erected below the castle ruins. When William Ewart Gladstone (he of the "bag" as much as one of Queen Victoria's Prime Ministers) married Catherine Glynne he acquired the estate and lived there for some sixty years. Gladstone is still commemorated by a museum, memorial windows and a library. As far as I know he was not a golfer or he might have laid out a course in the grounds long before Hawarden Golf Club was founded in 1911.

It is a pretty course, gentle parkland for the most part, quite different from the uncompromising links, ball-swallowing heathland or out-and-out mountaineering further west. You will find it just off the old main road beyond the station, and until the last few years its nine holes ran back and forth quite gently there. But recent advantage has been taken of the availability of a parcel of land on the other side of the railway line and a full 18-hole layout is now in play, the new holes being no less full of character than the originals. The club not only granted me access to play in the course of my researches but also very graciously allowed my teenage son to accompany me. We have not had so much fun for quite a long time.

The fun starts right at the outset with an intriguing 1st hole played from an elevated tee over a ravine and up to a hilltop landing site. Here the fairway turns to the left through 90° before plunging down steeply towards the green on the far side of a ditch. No less attractive is the short par-3 2nd across another valley to a ledge green.

Then it is time for the first of the new holes working its way down beside the railway to a green squeezed between the rails on one side and an ever-encroaching fence on the right. I should not like to have to hit a *spoon* shot in to this green too often. A path leads under the railway to the 4th tee and if you have not driven too well so far the view here will fill you with trepidation. It is not merely enough to reach the far side of the chasm immediately in front of the tee. Neither must you tangle with the trees on either hand. In an ideal world you will hope to make good progress up the rising fairway far in front for the approach shot may be blind and the green is perilously close to the railway on the right.

Now matters ease a little with a gentle pitch down to the short 5th and plenty of room on the ensuing drives, though it needs accuracy as well as length to bring the 6th green in range of two shots with the green on a promontory and a deceptive ridge in front. The screw is tightened, so to speak, on the 8th, the first of consecutive "Signature holes", the drive complicated by the need to keep the ball on the left of the fairway and a big tree occupying that ideal spot. Then it is a meaty carry not only over a pond but also up the bank on the far side to a two-tier amphitheatre green.

I hate that term, "Signature hole". It is to golf course architecture what "In need of some modernisation" is to estate agency or "One careful lady owner" to dealing in second-hand cars. The 9th at Hawarden is better qualified to have the term applied than most, a real exercise in brinkmanship. From the hilltop tee all is clearly visible below, most prominently the stream which interrupts the fairway. A well-judged tee shot reaches the flatter ground at the bottom of the hill yet stops without trickling into the stream. The second shot needs equal precision with a hedge close on the right and a duck pond on the left of the narrow green.

The 10th is at least as full of excitement and altogether tougher beginning with a drive returning over the same ponds and ditches we have just been trying to avoid. The length and position of the drive are limited by the last of the ditches beyond which the fairway climbs steeply past bunkers to the green. The 11th continues the climb and ends the run of new holes.

Back under the railway line the 12th is a roly-poly par-5 climbing two hills and curving all the time to the right. Its green introduces play to a softer kind of parkland over which a score ought to be consolidated before essaying the final two holes, the 17th needing a long second shot over a deceptive depression if par is to be achieved in regulation fashion. All the good work so far may easily be undone on the 18th, a gorgeous hole, but horribly treacherous. From an elevated tee there is a mere window in the trees giving a view of the little green far below, bunkers eating into the putting surface. The out-of-bounds fence runs awfully close on the left and a fast-flowing stream cuts across the front on the diagonal. In a swirling wind the hole is a siren. Who needs a Standard Scratch Score of 75 when 68 can give so much enjoyment to a lad and his father?

*(MR)*

| Card of the course: | | | | | |
|---|---|---|---|---|---|
| 1. | 315 yards | par 4 | 10. | 405 yards | par 4 |
| 2. | 157 | 3 | 11. | 156 | 3 |
| 3. | 380 | 4 | 12. | 490 | 5 |
| 4. | 372 | 4 | 13. | 369 | 4 |
| 5. | 118 | 3 | 14. | 132 | 3 |
| 6. | 400 | 4 | 15. | 381 | 4 |
| 7. | 477 | 5 | 16. | 378 | 4 |
| 8. | 388 | 4 | 17. | 421 | 4 |
| 9. | 386 | 4 | 18. | 169 | 3 |
| Out: | 2993 yards | par 35 | | | |
| In: | 2901 yards | par 34 | | | |
| Total: | 5894 yards | par 69 | s.s.s. 68 | | |

# Holyhead

*6050 yards; par 71; s.s.s. 70*

I was first aware of Holyhead when I was a fanatical train spotter, as a youngster spending many hours on the platforms of Crewe Station seeking the numbers and names of the majestic steam engines including those which transported thousands of people from the capital to the extremities of the Isle of Anglesey. (Memories of Royal Scots, Patriots, Jubilees and Black Fives!) The port and holiday centre of Holyhead is truly at the end of the run of the important cross-country A5 trunk route and the town still plays a significant communication rôle as an Irish sea ferry port.

Holyhead is located on the small Holy Island on which is scattered a profusion of ancient sites. The rugged Holyhead Mountain drops severely to the sea in spectacular fashion while South Stack, the westernmost tip of the island, is a rocky promontory crowned with a lighthouse and as famous for its seabird colonies as it is for its scenery.

The golf course is on the outskirts of Holyhead at Trearddur Bay. It is a challenging heathland course and enjoys scenic views down the coast to the Menai Straits and to Snowdonia beyond. The course, like so many in North Wales, was designed by James Braid in 1912 and as is customary of his designs there is an excellent mix of holes to relish. However, I was somewhat surprised at the number of bunkers no longer in existence.

There is nothing more inviting than a wide-open fairway, hazard free for the first drive of the day. This is certainly *not* the case at Holyhead! A relatively short par-4 with out-of-bounds and gorse to its left, the 1st can create early havoc. Most courses have a hole which long remains in the mind and here it is the 2nd with a vast depression to carry and out-of-bounds again to the left. If that is not enough to bring on the "white-knuckle" syndrome there is the sheerest of drops to the right side of the green.

After the 3rd, which is a par-5 full of peaks and troughs to a plateau green, the par-3 4th is played from an elevated tee which is awkwardly angled in relation to the wide but

**Holyhead 4th & 3rd**

59

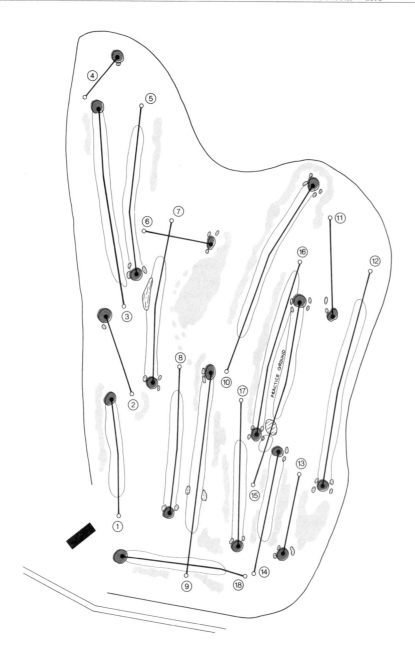

narrow green, leaving little to the imagination, but how I long for the return of a once astutely placed bunker in front of the green! The slight dog-leg 5th, with its narrow fairway difficult to define, does not go without its problems and the green is well protected. With three par-3s in the first six holes the 6th would appear to be the most sporting. Bushes and rocky outcrops to the side and beyond the green tend to foreshorten the hole.

An excellent par-4 follows with a pond to the right and a crag corner to the left. The first time player can easily be intimidated on the tee but the problems do not end there. The pond feeds into a ditch on the right of the fairway and a slick and well-guarded green can easily take its toll. Heading down the 8th towards the club house the emphasis is on a well-placed tee shot. Anything hit too far left makes for a second shot which is blind and difficult to judge.

When alterations take place on any golf hole they invariably become the talking point both during play and over a beer in the club house. I am sure the change to the 9th, once a gruelling par-4, now a par-5, is no exception and in my opinion it is still a very good golf hole, with an abundance of gorse, large mounds and bunkers to contend with. Without making too much of an issue of the reduction of bunkers on the course, this is now the only hole, with the exception of the par-3s, on which bunkers play their part in arresting inaccurate tee shots.

The 10th, a fascinating hole just a few yards longer than the minimum requirement for a par-5, is a beauty. The drive, with its carry over a mass of gorse to a narrowing fairway, can leave all sorts of indecision over the second shot. A well-played fairway wood avoiding gorse and rocks will be rewarded with the simplest of pitch shots to the green. The next, invariably a wood shot from the tee, is void of greenside protection.

The longest of the par-5s is the 12th, with out-of-bounds flanking the left side of the fairway for its complete length, and it offers vast room down the right for the drive. Holyhead possesses several splendid short holes and the 13th is an example. It is downhill, surrounded by gorse bushes and has four greenside bunkers. Par is not easily achieved by the wayward! Then comes a short, but intriguing, par-4 playing uphill through a corridor of gorse and rock. The first substantial par-4 is the 15th with its tee nestling high up on a rocky outcrop amongst gorse. It offers little comfort to an errant shot left as the practice ground is deemed out-of-bounds but there are acres of space to the right making for an ideal baling out area when you have a good card on the go.

With three holes to play, the 16th, with its generously wide fairway and gently downhill approach, is in stark contrast to the penultimate hole. The drive is played from amongst thick gorse to the top of a hill and beyond. Then comes the decision either to fly the ball into the heart of the green or to play a low pitch-and-run down the severely sloping fairway. A word of warning! Overshoot the green and the deftest of touches is needed for the return pitch.

It is a daunting tee shot on the final hole with out-of-bounds and gorse plus a severe right-to-left sloping fairway over its early stages. Successful negotiation will leave you with a straightforward iron shot to the plateau Mackenzie green. The course, in benign conditions, makes for a most enjoyable round and a fair test of golf but when the winds gust from the Irish Sea it is a very different ball game high on the Anglesey headland.

*(PL)*

### Card of the course:

| No. | Yards | Par | No. | Yards | Par |
|-----|-------|-----|-----|-------|-----|
| 1. | 277 yards | par 4 | 10. | 478 yards | par 5 |
| 2. | 180 | 3 | 11. | 226 | 3 |
| 3. | 479 | 5 | 12. | 517 | 5 |
| 4. | 124 | 3 | 13. | 177 | 3 |
| 5. | 391 | 4 | 14. | 268 | 4 |
| 6. | 154 | 3 | 15. | 416 | 4 |
| 7. | 376 | 4 | 16. | 448 | 4 |
| 8. | 337 | 4 | 17. | 343 | 4 |
| 9. | 476 | 5 | 18. | 383 | 4 |
| Out: | 2794 yards | par 35 | | | |
| In: | 3256 yards | par 36 | | | |
| Total: | 6050 yards | par 71 | | s.s.s. 70 | |

# Holywell

*6073 yards; par 70; s.s.s. 70*

One talks of Ganton as being an inland links, Walton Heath, too, even though it is at least 40 miles from the English Channel. They both feel and play like seaside courses. Exactly the same could be said of Holywell, 800 feet up on the moors. It has that wonderfully crisp, fast-running turf you expect to find only within earshot of breaking surf. I played the course in torrential rain and can vouch for the exceptional drainage of the underlying limestone. The wind, which is rarely absent from such an upland site, also does its bit to ensure good conditions under foot and firm fairway lies.

They will be thinking about their Centenary celebrations any day now, for the club dates back to 1906 and soon ran to 18 holes up towards the monument you can see from the A55. (You may also have caught a glimpse of the course as you sped along the dual-carriageway but what you saw was quite unlike the rest of the course). Wartime military needs and the talk of road improvements reduced the course to 9 holes, but in 1991, when the road had been completed, Holywell once again became an 18-hole layout. The views in clear weather are stirring, south and west towards Moel Fammau and the Clwydian range, and for the lover of traditional golf the first sighting of the course itself raises the spirits. Slender ribbons of fairway thread an unsteady course through a crumpled landscape, an occasional flag peeping out from rocky outcrops, gorse bushes and encircling battlements of earthworks, the vestiges of the lead mining which once took place here.

*Holywell 15th*

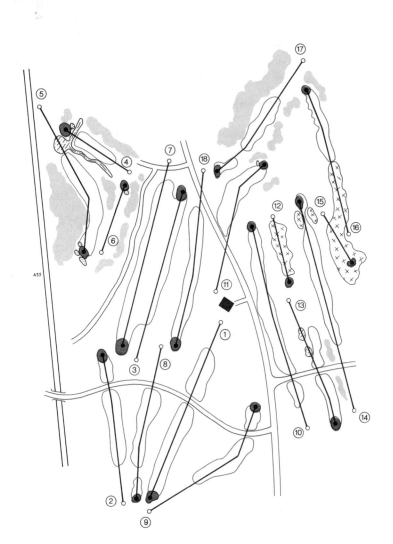

The first experience of Holywell's fine turf comes with the opening drive, the fairway running expansively out to a sloping green. You were unlucky if you tangled with the little crater which sits in the middle of the fairway about 150 yards out, but you will have to get used to them for they proliferate over the back nine. There is a change of character on the 2nd, a recently created hole on meadowland turf, and the 3rd gives an opportunity to open the shoulders. However, it is worth reminding yourself of the local rules printed on the scorecard before playing each hole for there are several instances when out-of-bounds threatens and, though you will be a long way off course if you sin on the 3rd, you may like to note the markers for when you return up the 7th.

Passing through an iron gate, the nature of the course changes and it is worth studying the plan of the 4th hole helpfully displayed by the tee before selecting your club. In front of the green is a ditch and to the left a small pond. This is a far more exacting hole when viewed from the tee than it appears to be from the comfort of a passing automobile! Driving back over the pond, from the 5th tee, you must make a fair distance in the direction of the marker post if you hope to get a sight of the green, otherwise much research is required in determining the precise line and distance for the second shot, the green hidden away behind a tree-covered mound and well protected by bunkers. (How cheering, in April, to find the bank behind the green ablaze with blooming daffodils!). The 6th completes this loop, a mid-iron to a green ringed with trees. Each of these three holes had at least one bunker. There will be only one more on the rest of the course, but on wild moorland there are perils of a more punitive kind.

The long 7th returns to this moorland, a fine hole with deceptive lower ground before the green tempting you to take insufficient club to reach the putting surface. No topping from now on! The 8th is the first of a succession of holes teeing off over unpredictable bumpy ground, though its fairway is meadow-like. The sight of the approach shot clearing further uneven ground on the run in to the green is satisfying. So, too, is the drive which makes good distance and avoids the out-of-bounds on the 9th, the green on the far side of a minor road.

The first par-5 of the round follows, a hole on which it is possible to drift right into ponds in an effort to avoid the out-of-bounds road along the left of the fairway. Beginning at this hole there is little point in trying to record each significant hollow and hump which may interfere with your golf. On this side of the road the ground tumbles about wildly and you are going to experience a good many "sporting" lies before the end of the round.

It is a longish walk past the clubhouse to the 11th tee, but this provides a suitable alternative starting point right outside the Secretary's office (so God help you if you have dawdled on the round so far!). The tee-shot is across the road to a fairway curving to the right and climbing to a crinkled green amidst bumpy ground, bushes and the final bunker of the round. The 12th is not long, but directly into a strong wind it took a full 3-iron shot to carry not only rough ground but also a big mound directly in front of the green, and that from the yellow markers!

Holywell is proud of the diversity of its holes and the thought-provoking nature of so many of them. The 13th is a cape-hole which causes you to consider how much to attempt to carry. The direct line is out over a couple of ponds and some very unpleasant rough. If you err on the side of safety you might find yourself in a number of small trees on the left of the fairway put there to prevent your taking that route. There is a tidy carry, as well, over gorse from the 14th tee with a quarry on the right. The green on this hole is in its own gathering dell, as if had been transported here direct from Lahinch.

A diminutive green awaits on the 15th and if you miss it you are in frightful trouble, the green being the only hospitable spot in the wilderness of a quarry. The view from the medal tee on the 16th is at least as intimidating, with an apparently endless carry over further excavations to a distant marker post. In fact the distance is not as great as it seems and a long-iron might be the prudent club to take with a menacing sequence of craters perforating the fairway on the left. There are two more craters right in front of the green to add needle to the pitch.

There are probably as many different strategies on how to play the 17th as there are ways to make yourself look foolish. It is a shortish par-4 that really needs no more than a mid-iron to find the level fairway in front of the marker post followed by another weighted to run with the slope of the land onto the narrow, angled green. There are ball-swallowing bushes to ensnare the drive (you could even fail to clear the cairn in front of the tee) and the ground is very uneven as the fairway bears right after the marker post. It is also quite possible to ping-pong back and forth across the narrowest part of the green as your chipping is tested by the grassy hollows abutting the green. Then it is time to launch a big drive from the final tee, the fairway rising to a crest before falling gently towards the green.

Those there are — well-known professionals especially — who dislike links golf because they might not get a perfect lie after a 350-yard drive. In contrast, I well remember the son of a respected teaching-professional, a county player, practising pitches from a metalled road. He had just been thoroughly tested at Saunton and understood full well the uncertainties of the real game as played on a proper links course. You have to be able to improvise when your lie is not quite as you might have hoped. The truly skilled golfer will adapt his game, or invent new shots, to cope with novel lies. At Holywell improvisation is likely to be required many times during the round. It is under such circumstances that the best players demonstrate their superior skills.

*(MR)*

### Card of the course:

| | | | | | |
|---|---|---|---|---|---|
| 1. | 397 yards | par 4 | 10. | 480 yards | par 5 |
| 2. | 331 | 4 | 11. | 336 | 4 |
| 3. | 404 | 4 | 12. | 163 | 3 |
| 4. | 188 | 3 | 13. | 317 | 4 |
| 5. | 374 | 4 | 14. | 509 | 5 |
| 6. | 165 | 3 | 15. | 134 | 3 |
| 7. | 445 | 4 | 16. | 340 | 4 |
| 8. | 364 | 4 | 17. | 333 | 4 |
| 9. | 373 | 4 | 18. | 420 | 4 |
| Out: | 3041 yards | par 34 | | | |
| In: | 3032 yards | par 36 | | | |
| Total: | 6073 yards | par 70 | s.s.s. 70 | | |

# Kinsale Hall

*5944 yards; par 69; s.s.s. 69*

Driving along the old coast road from Queensferry to Prestatyn your eye is suddenly caught by what appears to be an ocean going liner berthed in the middle of a green field. If you turn inland from there, as if to the trout farm, you will immediately find the drive to Kinsale Hall. Passing across the front of the hotel you reach the golf course and from the car park there is a fine view down to the coast and, lo and behold, there is the liner in full view neither as large as it seemed at first nor berthed in the middle of the field but, rather, in a dock at the end of a causeway.

The very recent Kinsale course is a joint venture between

**Kinsale Hall 9th**

65

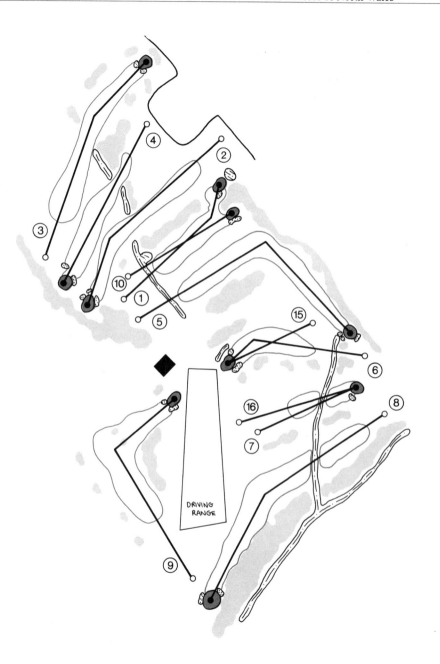

private owners and Flint County Council, and great credit they deserve for bringing golf in such surroundings and with so much character within reach of almost everybody's pocket. It is not intended in any way to be patronising when I say that you would never suspect there was municipal involvement, such is the style of the course and the general condition. There are plans to expand some day to 18 holes, but it will not be at the expense of the driving range which must be one of the most spectacular in existence, golfers hitting out down a steep hill towards the Dee Estuary, the Wirral beyond, and, of course, the said ship.

Do not rush up the steep hill to the 1st tee. Pace yourself! Once you are there the ground is merely gently sloping, the first 4½ holes working back and forth at the top of the hill. If you can keep your drives straight and out of the trees you will have no problems, though reading putts on these greens is not as easy as you might think. Several greens are stepped and all undulate, but the real problem is identifying which borrows are actually on the green and which are illusions caused by the general slope of the land. The outstanding ½-hole comes on the 5th, a huge par-4 on which you drive along the top of the hill before turning sharply right and steeply downhill to a green at the bottom. Big hitters may be tempted to cut off a bit of the dog-leg by smashing the ball out over the trees on the right but they will probably leave themselves with a steeply hanging lie from which to play to the green. However you play the hole, leave yourself time to admire the view over the sea to Hoylake and Hilbre Island – and, naturally enough, the same ship.

Variety was introduced as early as the 1st hole with separate 1st and 10th greens which, coupled with different tees, created a short par-4 and a long par-3. Much the same thing happens on the 6th/15th and 7th/16th. The former requires a drive played up the right to allow the slope to do its bit and leave a gentle pitch in to the green. The 7th is a straightforward par-3 downhill, but when the same hole is played as a 294-yard par-4 it is quite different, the drive needing to clear a ditch and, ideally, the worst of a big mound leaning into the fairway on the left. Walking down the steep, terraced hillside I was momentarily reminded of the vineyards high above the Rhône near Vienne – not at all what I might readily associate with Mostyn!

The 8th is a long slow curve and for most of us it is a bogey-5 with the slope on the fairway and the threat of trees and a stream on the left to make us play sensibly. As sharp a dog-leg as you are likely to find, the 9th works its way back uphill with a tree in the centre of the fairway the ideal line, as long as you don't then leave yourself stymied behind it. It is not an easy hole to get right first time out, but when you have played it once and have assessed the problems you will be able to plan your strategy for future rounds.

*(MR)*

| Card of the course: | | | | | |
|---|---|---|---|---|---|
| 1. | 261 yards | par 4 | 10. | 220 yards | par 3 |
| 2. | 320 | 4 | 11. | 320 | 4 |
| 3. | 364 | 4 | 12. | 364 | 4 |
| 4. | 305 | 4 | 13. | 307 | 4 |
| 5. | 461 | 4 | 14. | 461 | 4 |
| 6. | 267 | 4 | 15. | 166 | 3 |
| 7. | 184 | 3 | 16. | 294 | 4 |
| 8. | 446 | 4 | 17. | 446 | 4 |
| 9. | 379 | 4 | 18. | 379 | 4 |
| Out: | 2987 yards | par 35 | | | |
| In: | 2957 yards | par 34 | | | |
| Total: | 5944 yards | par 69 | | s.s.s. 69 | |

# Llanfairfechan

*3119 yards; par 54; s.s.s. 57*

This small seaside resort is laid out along a narrow coastal strip which is backed by steep-sided mountains. Its Victorian promenade which appears to have been untouched by time is a delight. The pleasantly situated hillside golf course with its exquisite views lies on the north boundary of the Snowdonia National Park, and 1996 is the 25th anniversary of this challenging par-3 course. It is difficult now to believe that in 1971 a 10-year husband and wife joint-membership was £50 (£2.50 per person per year) and a full male membership was £35 for 10 years, or £3.50 a year, and many of those original members were introduced to the sport by me when I held evening classes in the village hall.

A brook which runs through the course comes into play at

**Llanfairfechan 9th/18th**

various holes. Holes 3 and 12 put the tee shot to the test due to numerous sycamore trees situated across the fairway. The 15th, 210 yards all uphill to a plateau green, again calls for impressive tee play.

The 7th and 16th tee shots are played to a "cricket wicket" green, 22 yards long and 7 yards wide. The method of play can vary between a full, tossed lofted iron or a low punched long iron if faced with the south-westerly prevailing wind.

*(PL)*

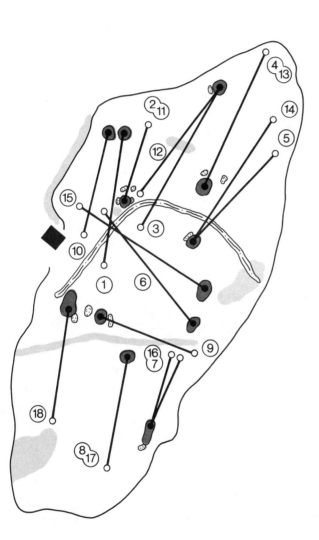

### Card of the course:

| 1. | 185 yards | par 3 | 10. | 170 yards | par 3 |
|----|-----------|-------|-----|-----------|-------|
| 2. | 119 | 3 | 11. | 119 | 3 |
| 3. | 238 | 3 | 12. | 207 | 3 |
| 4. | 215 | 3 | 13. | 215 | 3 |
| 5. | 169 | 3 | 14. | 202 | 3 |
| 6. | 215 | 3 | 15. | 210 | 3 |
| 7. | 111 | 3 | 16. | 118 | 3 |
| 8. | 164 | 3 | 17. | 164 | 3 |
| 9. | 140 | 3 | 18. | 158 | 3 |

| Out: | 1556 yards | par 27 | | |
|------|-----------|--------|---|---|
| In: | 1563 yards | par 27 | | |
| Total: | 3119 yards | par 54 | s.s.s. 57 | |

# Llangefni

*2974 yards; par 56*

In the winter months of the late '60s and early '70s my Friday evenings were invariably taken up journeying to the market town of Llangefni on the Island of Anglesey. Although there was no golf course, there was a nucleus of locals who were very keen to learn to play. The learning ground was the High School's gymnasium with its coconut mats and airflow balls. It was not until September 1983 that the wishes of many were granted when Llangefni's public golf course was opened.

The popularity of this course with its eight par-3s and solitary par-4 is immense. Set in parkland on the outskirts of the town, it is slightly undulating and has hedgerows dividing the holes. The two holes of interest are the well-trapped dog-leg 4th and the downhill 8th with its captivating views of the mountains in the distance.

*(PL)*

**Llangefni 3rd**

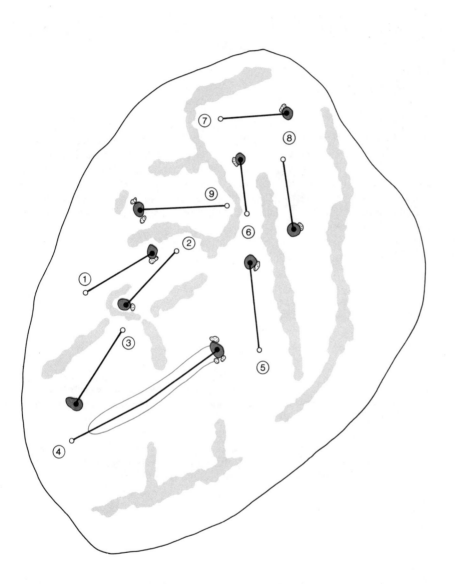

**Card of the course:**

| | | |
|---|---|---|
| 1. | 154 yards | par 3 |
| 2. | 133 | 3 |
| 3. | 151 | 3 |
| 4. | 328 | 4 |
| 5. | 158 | 3 |
| 6. | 99 | 3 |
| 7. | 152 | 3 |
| 8. | 138 | 3 |
| 9. | 174 | 3 |
| Out: | 1487 yards | par 28 |
| Total: | 2974 yards | par 56 |

# Llanymynech

*6114 yards; par 70; s.s.s. 69*

As I sat on the bench below the 10th tee waiting my turn to play my thoughts turned to that great eclectic course in the sky. There was Henry Longhurst presiding over proceedings as Old Tom Morris, Harry Vardon and Bob Jones essayed *Amen Corner* (on the *Eden Course* here), *The Monk*, *The Cardinal* and, to end, *Perfection*. They were, naturally enough, spared the vulgar indignities of *Hell Bunker*, *Bloody Bidet* and *The Devil's Chair*. If such ramblings may be thought out of place in a book such as this, if only geographically, I ought to add that I was at Llanymynech on the last Friday of October under a sun which would not have been out of place in June, the trees turning through every shade of amber and gold, the clearest and bluest of skies below which to view most of Wales and a very large part of England, and the course in grand condition. Heaven indeed on earth!

There are many less celestial reasons to visit Llanymynech. You may, for instance, be a historian seeking out the sites of Caractacus or walking Offa's Dyke. You may be a golfing pilgrim wishing to tread the very turf in which the juvenile Ian Woosnam left his spike marks. You may simply like to test those parts of your golfing technique unlikely to be examined by a lowland layout. If you are not at peace with your driver bring a plentiful supply of spare balls.

Llanymynech is the second golf club to utilise this particular site which it has done since the 1930s. Formerly it was home to the Oswestry club and Llanymynech is able to take advantage of dual nationality, the England-Wales border running through the course. The clubhouse is firmly in Wales and, before going out to play, take a look at the card of Ian Woosnam's course record 65 hanging there and also the remarkable montage of photographs showing the full 360° panorama visible from the highest point.

The nature of the course will come as no surprise: the narrow lane leading up to the club from the village of Pant climbs vigorously and crosses the 2nd fairway on the way in. So you are prepared for the tricky par-3 which opens the round, played across a dip to a very exposed green protected by a mound on the right and giving fine views of the Shropshire plain to the east and Rodney's Pillar and the Breidden Hills further to the south. Then driving across the road on the 2nd there is a big slope down to the right which dictates that all shots must be aimed well left to finish centrally.

You may have to play over (or through) trees on the short 3rd and trees will be a major factor over the next half dozen holes. Certainly you are required to know just how much woodland you can carry from the 4th tee, the fairway a sharp dog-leg to the left with no safe option on the outside of the curve. A plaque by the tee indicates that you

*Drive in WALES*
*Putt out in ENGLAND.*

Those who feel that this book should concern itself solely with Welsh golf may prefer to rejoin the narrative on the 7th tee, beginning at the next paragraph. In truth the 4th green is rather pretty, set off against a low stone wall backed by mature woods. The 5th is of similar length but this time there is less to be gained by corner-cutting as the second shot is required to climb over some very bumpy ground to find the elevated green. I doubt the famed fall in New England could be any finer than the autumn trees which framed this hole on the day of my visit. From a high tee up behind this green there is a lovely falling shot to the 6th, with a mound on the right and the general slope tending to throw the ball down the hill to the left.

Returning to Wales, there is another high platform tee on the 7th, well exposed to the wind, and a long drive is called for as the next shot is played uphill to the green. However, in striving for length, it is important not to pull the ball to the left into the ditch separating this fairway from the next. That might be preferable, though, to a wild slice for live World War II shells were found very recently only just over the fence!

Not only is the ditch very much in mind as you play from the 8th tee but also you need to ensure that you do not run out of fairway where it turns sharply up the hill to the right. (Perhaps you made a note of the pin position as you crossed the valley when playing the 3rd.) Then the 9th climbs gently but persistently as it winds its lengthy way into the wind. Trees now give way to gorse and bracken and the final approach is likely to be blind – and how deceptive these greens can be! So often the extreme slopes of surrounding hills deceive the eye giving the impression that the greens are dead level. I doubt if there is anything approaching a flat green at Llanymynech.

The back nine begins as the outward half does with a par-3, this one rather sterner with a long carry across a gully, two bunkers on the right and terrible trouble away to the left. Matters are made no simpler by the hole's exposure to the wind and the difficulty of choosing the correct club. Beyond, on the 11th tee, you wait for the bell to signal that the green is clear before driving blind over a marker post. On a still day your next shot might be a putt, but into

*Llanymynech 7th*

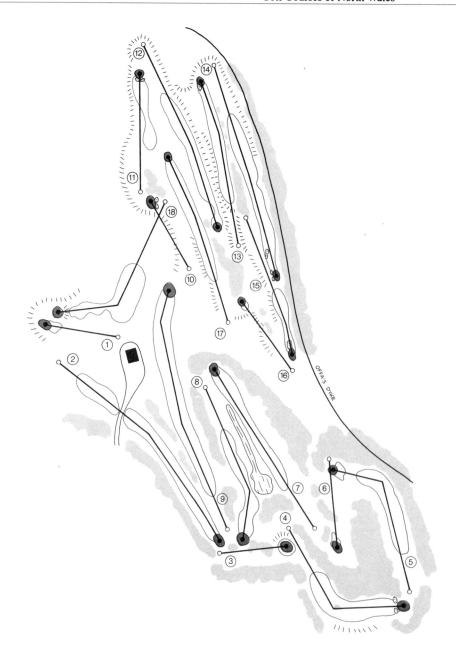

the wind you may well find yourself having to play a tricky pitch from a downhill lie between bunkers to a tiny, sloping green.

At last we have reached the 12th tee, which is to Llanymynech what the 4th green is to Welshpool, a few miles down the road. Simply it is right on top of a pinnacle with quite stupendous views all round. Apparently seven of the old Welsh counties are visible from it making the narrow ribbon of fairway seem even more slender. (I could not help but reflect that this tee – particularly the back one – is designed to ensure a full forward transfer of weight as you drive. Were you to stagger backwards you might end up a few hundred feet lower than expected). Miss the fairway on the left and your ball is lost down the mountainside. Though it may seem safer on the right you will be lucky if you can get out of the rough cleanly enough to make it over the ridge just beyond which the green sits under its marker post. You would, I imagine, prefer not to have to approach the green from this angle for there is a huge drop on the left only a few feet from the putting surface.

The 13th fairway is very inviting from the tee which clings to the hillside far above. Ideally you hug as close as you dare the steep slopes on the left in order to finish centrally. Even from there the next shot is tricky to judge up and over an angled ridge to a sloping green. Running back parallel, the 14th fairway keeps company with Offa's Dyke on the left, though of greater golfing consequence are the trees on either side. If you find the middle of the fairway you may well have a realistic chance of reaching the green in two for the fairway grass is links-like and gives plenty of roll plus, on the whole, decent lies for clean striking. Three bunkers of a seaside nature await the faded approach.

There is a bunker that would not be out of place at St. Andrews on the 15th. You cannot see it from the tee for, once again, you are driving towards a marker post on top of a ridge. Were you to clear the ridge (and many drives do) your ball would very probably race down the other side into *"a cavern dark enough to mask thy monstrous visage"* (*Julius Caesar*). On this terrain few bunkers are needed, those there are employed tellingly.

We have regained the shelter of the woods, yet almost immediately we rejoin the battle with the wind on the 16th, uphill and most likely straight into the teeth of the gale. Often we will be reaching for wood here. Certainly we will need two very good strikes to climb to the 17th green into the wind. But it is not just a matter of distance for the fairway is narrow, there is a big drop on the left while a jungle of bushes and briars covers the hill on the right.

Finally there is an inspiring drive from a hillside tee (albeit very much in range of inaccurate 10th tee shots) down into a punchbowl in front of the clubhouse. If you are feeling strong you might risk trying the direct route but there is all manner of trouble should you fall short. There may be greater merit in finding a good lie on the far side of the punch-bowl from which there is a sight of the green.

That green is raised up proudly on its plateau surveying a most enormous expanse of handsome and unspoiled countryside, for centuries the scene of the bloodiest of battles:

*"The gale, it plies the saplings double*
*It blows so hard, 'twill soon be gone:*
*To-day the Romans and his trouble*
*Are ashes under Uricon."*

(A.E.Housman)

(MR)

## Card of the course:

| No. | Distance | Par | No. | Distance | Par |
|---|---|---|---|---|---|
| 1. | 164 yards | par 3 | 10. | 178 yards | par 3 |
| 2. | 532 | 5 | 11. | 260 | 4 |
| 3. | 164 | 3 | 12. | 438 | 4 |
| 4. | 357 | 4 | 13. | 369 | 4 |
| 5. | 363 | 4 | 14. | 487 | 5 |
| 6. | 198 | 3 | 15. | 320 | 4 |
| 7. | 416 | 4 | 16. | 189 | 3 |
| 8. | 359 | 4 | 17. | 392 | 4 |
| 9. | 544 | 5 | 18. | 384 | 4 |

| | | |
|---|---|---|
| Out: | 3097 yards | par 35 |
| In: | 3017 yards | par 35 |
| Total: | 6114 yards | par 70 | s.s.s. 69 |

# Maesdu

*6485 yards; par 72; s.s.s. 72*

Llandudno is, for many, the perfect vision of a seaside resort untainted by garishness: indeed, it has the appearance and feel of a genteel age. The wide promenade is backed by elegant Victorian façades and is framed by the cliffs of the Great and Little Ormes. The resort can boast two fine golf courses, Maesdu and North Wales.

The name, Maesdu (black field), dates back to 1098 A.D. when the Norwegians attacked and the bloody battle of Deganwy ensued on this very spot. More than 800 years later, in 1915, Llandudno Council allocated the land for a municipal golf course, the first municipal course in Wales. It was originally designed by Harry Colt (of Sunningdale fame) and later extended and improved by

**Maesdu 16th**

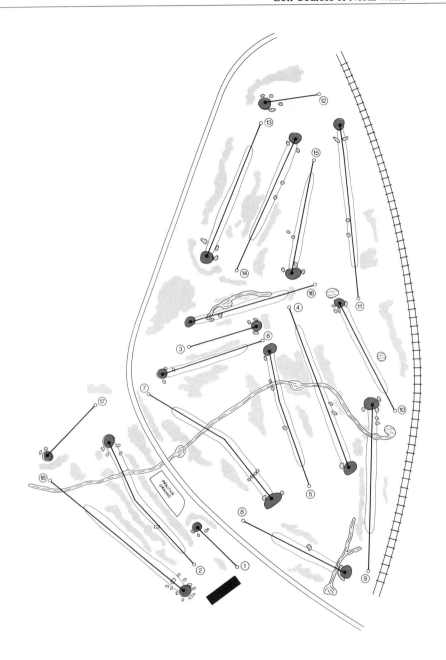

that great ambassador for professional golf, Tom Jones, the club's first and longest serving professional of some 52 years, with the help of fellow professional, Fred Collins. Not only did the course encourage tourism, but it became a venue for top professional tournaments in the 1950s and '60s: the Penfold Tournament was held here regularly, and winners included Peter Alliss, Henry Cotton, Harry Weetman, Peter Butler and Harry Bradshaw. This parkland course, situated on the gentle west-facing slopes of the Creuddyn Peninsula, provides a memorable and challenging experience. The magnificent views of the Conwy estuary, mountains of Snowdonia and the distant Menai Straits add to the attractions.

The opening hole, although not long, does not go without its difficulties with out-of-bounds to the right and a green which is both uphill and sloping from right to left. The 2nd, originally a par-5, has recently become a brute of a par-4. It is a slight dog-leg with trees either side of the fairway and out-of-bounds to the right. However, the main stumbling-block is a ditch across the fairway some 330 yards from the tee. Four bunkers, astutely placed just short of an undulating green, punish a wayward shot.

Now it is across the road, to a grand, slightly downhill, par-3 dependent on the force of the prevailing south-westerly wind, the hole playing anything from a long-iron to a full-blooded drive. The demanding 4th, uphill with a pond and another stretch of ditch to cope with, gives little respite and wayward shots which drift left into the line of trees are severely punished.

At last there is a not overlong, downhill, par-4, and what a beauty it is with its three strategically placed bunkers, the first of which is positioned on the left side of the fairway but that really is the line to take in order to get a clear view of the green. More trees and water come into play towards the latter part of the fairway. Nor is the tree-lined, shortish par-4 6th a doddle with its well-protected sloping green.

The next hole, the 7th, is a most demanding par-4 with the tee shot played close to the roadside with, yet again, the ditch to contend with. As the hole progresses a quartet of bunkers strewn across the fairway is perfectly placed to penalise all but truly struck second shots. The 8th is one of those unique holes the character of which is entirely dictated by the lie of the land (and the railway only just through the back of the green). It is a relatively short par-4 with innovations in the form of a pond and a ditch, the latter crossing the fairway on the approach to the green, thus making the big hitter think twice about club selection from the tee to this fast, sweeping fairway. Its awkwardly angled green used to be fronted by three bunkers. They have recently been made into a single monster. The effect is much the same: only a well-weighted pitch shot will make and hold the putting surface.

Holes 9, 10, and 11 run parallel with the railway line which divides the two Llandudno courses and they can seem awesome with yet more water hazards and the dreaded out-of-bounds on the right stretching the full length of all three holes. How many historic championship links courses enjoy the company of a railway line for at least some of the play! Situated at the furthest point from the club-house the short 12th, with its slightly elevated, tricky green, surrounded by four bunkers, requires a keen eye to judge the distance correctly.

No. 13 "unlucky for some" can be just that on this uphill and downdale hole. Bushes, thick rough and well-placed bunkers can take their toll. (Incidentally many Conwy players on the far side of the estuary take aim at this fairway if playing semi-blind to their 7th green).

The next, and in my opinion the best, hole on the course punishes a weak and wayward tee shot with gorse bushes both left and right of the fairway. A soundly struck tee shot is duly rewarded with a wide open and clear view of the low-lying green as well as the glorious scenery across the West Shore and over the Conwy estuary. The 15th is hardly an overly long par-4 but it has cunningly placed bunkers both for the tee shot and the approach to the cleverly designed green.

With just three holes to play and a good card on the go the next hole can be soul destroying with trees, water, and – again – very well-positioned bunkers to contend with. I have always found it a hole which seems to play longer than the card's yardage. Back across the main road from Deganwy to Llandudno is the relatively straightforward par-3 17th, albeit uphill.

With the club-house in the distance the eye-catching last hole plays from a an elevated tee with a carry of some 190 yards over a *Beechers Brook*-type obstacle stretching across the fairway. With out-of-bounds to the right and ten bunkers to contend with all positioned within 93 yards of the green this hole makes for a nerve-jangling finale to a golf course which has held not only the professional tournaments I mentioned earlier but also an abundance of top amateur events.

*(PL)*

### Card of the course:

| | | | | | |
|---|---|---|---|---|---|
| 1. | 140 yards | par 3 | 10. | 339 yards | par 4 |
| 2. | 450 | 4 | 11. | 492 | 5 |
| 3. | 203 | 3 | 12. | 155 | 3 |
| 4. | 513 | 5 | 13. | 413 | 4 |
| 5. | 390 | 4 | 14. | 427 | 4 |
| 6. | 305 | 4 | 15. | 331 | 4 |
| 7. | 455 | 4 | 16. | 387 | 4 |
| 8. | 323 | 4 | 17. | 199 | 3 |
| 9. | 476 | 5 | 18. | 487 | 5 |
| Out: | 3255 yards | par 36 | | | |
| In: | 3230 yards | par 36 | | | |
| Total: | 6485 yards | par 72 | | s.s.s. 72 | |

# Mold

*5528 yards; par 67; s.s.s. 67*

As a town, Mold dates from Norman times – *Montalt* or *Mons Alto* meaning "high mountain" and the Welsh *Gwyddgrug* equating to "mound". Before that there were Romano-British settlements and Iron Age hill forts and amongst Bronze Age remains from the area was a magnificent gold cape discovered in the 1830s and now in the British Museum. In 447 A.D. a small number of Christian Britons called upon Bishop Germanus of Auxerre to help them fight a large force of pagan Picts and Saxons. Encouraged by Germanus they shouted "Alleluia" over and over again in a hollow surrounded by hills and their shouts echoed to such effect that the pagans fled, fearing they were facing a vast army. There is a monument commemorating this battle at Maes Garmon between Mold and Gwernaffield on the west of the town. Out there, too, at Pantymwyn is Mold Golf Club, and if you have time after your round it is worth exploring the maze of little roads around here, the countryside and villages very pretty in the evening sun.

The Golf Club is thought to have started on Hafod Moor in 1909, moving then to Padeswood, and finally settling at Pantymwyn in 1928. A second-hand cricket pavilion was acquired and this moved with the club from site to site remaining in use right up until the 1960s! Only 36 acres were needed to accommodate the 1928 course, the indigenous hazards including limestone walls, hawthorn hedges, and gorse while the fairways were described in the club's 75th Anniversary handbook as "nothing more than sheep pasture, rocky, covered with outcrops and showing the relics of lead mining." The history from then has been one of gradual expansion and improvement, beginning with water and toilets. Later came the instigation of Sunday play. It was not until after World War II that electric lighting was acquired and only in the late 1950s did members at the Annual General Meeting vote in favour of the club's having a bar. The cricket pavilion was eventually replaced and in the 1970s the course was expanded to a full 18 holes. There have been many changes to the layout even since then

and under the consultancy of Hawtrees further improvements are being undertaken as I write, not only to increase the challenge for competent golfers but also to improve safety and assist course maintenance. I played here with the Club Treasurer and frequently as my drive finished on the side of a fairway he would say, "There'll be a bunker there next time you come!"

Mold is a compact course, somewhere about 90 acres now, and six par-3s contribute to the modest overall length. Do not be misled, however, into thinking this is a small course! A plateau of high ground occupies the centre of the course and several very substantial holes, notably the 7th, 15th and 18th, climb to the plateau, run along it for some way, and finally plunge down the far side to the green, rather like playing a brontosaurus from nose to tail. It would be an unusual course on which no hole bore any resemblance to another (Wrexham, perhaps?) but it is fair to say that Mold packs a great deal more variety and interest into its 5,500 yards than many a meadowland course 1,000 yards longer. When Hawtrees have finished there will be even more character to Mold, and only the most accurate of golfers will tame it.

As new land has been acquired so the order of the holes has been changed, and the round now starts down below the car park, the fairway climbing steadily as trees restrict the width. Even after a good drive the pitch is tricky to judge with the green raised up behind a slight ridge. You will be tempted to launch a drive far into the distance on the downhill 2nd, a big tree in the middle of the fairway more than likely thwarting you in the attempt. If you aim too far to the side of the tree your angled approach shot will be made more difficult by further trees and the worst ignominy is to find you have no shot at all because you are right up against the trunk. One of the recently added holes, the 3rd, is deceptive, bunkered in such a way that the green appears closer than it really is. With the additional effect of the hill to take into account you will need a good deal more club than you might imagine.

A stately cherry tree in mid-fairway plus bunkers on the right and a hedge on the left tighten the 4th drive markedly. The hole runs uphill, too, so 288 yards play more like 350 and, with lively bunkering around the green, you will not want to have to improvise your approach shot from under branches. The 5th is bunkerless yet capable of punishing the wayward severely, first on the drive with out-of-bounds trees on the right, and then on the pitch, with a big drop into a wilderness just through the back of the triangular green.

The side of the hill on the left eats into the fairway in such a way that if the hole is cut on the very left of the green you have no shot to it unless you have placed your drive accurately in the right half of the fairway. The green used to be slightly further to the right but, having been constructed on an old lead working, one day it just caved in!

The second short hole, the 6th, is a lovely drop shot across gorse and from a tee low down beside this green you are required to hit

*Mold 6th*

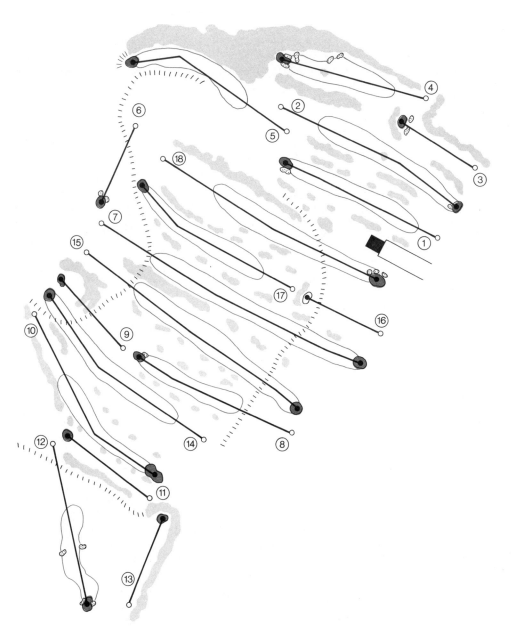

a long drive high enough to climb above the rock face in front of you to find the 7th fairway. You could get up there with a 7-iron, but somehow pride always wins over common sense and out comes the flat-faced driver! Assuming you have no problem with the combination of height and distance, take care not to drift right into the bushes lying in wait or over the out-of-bounds wall. This is the first of the "brontosaurus" holes. The 8th also starts with an uphill drive, but on this occasion the green is a plateau at the end of the high ground, and not one to overshoot. In the Hawtree plan a slight hump just in front of the green is to be taken out so that a truly hit approach is not deflected to one side or the other. Raising of the green is imminent on the 9th in the said plan and it has been whispered that a watercarry may be part of the strategy. With no elevation and the only water that falling as rain the green nevertheless proved remarkably elusive to us.

Play returns to the highest part of the course on the 10th and in clear weather you can see past Helsby and Frodsham as far as the Peak District to the east, northwards up to the coast at Rhyl, and west to Moel Fammau and the hills of the Clwydian Range. After the short 11th (not a hole on which to develop a hook) the 12th drives out from a lofty tee to a fairway far below. With out-of-bounds to the left and fairway bunkers on either side this is not quite the trifle the card may suggest. Climbing the hill to the 13th green is currently a matter of club selection, but it will be trickier when Hawtree has finished with it.

By now you will be at home playing down to greens from the central plateau and you will be glad of the previous practice when essaying the approach to the 14th. You get another chance to execute the same skills on the 15th which runs parallel to the 7th, involves many of the same problems and is almost the same length, only this time it qualifies as a par-4 – a very tough one, Stroke 1 amongst several stringent tests.

The 16th really ought to be nothing, a poke up the hill with a short iron, except that the distance must be judged absolutely correctly. Fall short by only a few inches and the ball rolls a long way back towards you. The Hawtree plan envisages bunkers to penalise further those who are found wanting. There is respite of a sort on the 17th, a none-too-long par-4 along the plateau towards the stone hut by the 6th tee, but from there an intimidating drive must be made on the 18th. This hole has been altered recently to play to a new green short of the old one, not least to save most of us the embarrassment of hitting the clubhouse directly on the roof with our second shots. A new teeing ground has been constructed further back and it is possible that the new hole will play to a length of over 470 yards yet still remain within the parameters of par-4.

Wherever the tee finally settles, the drive is made to a narrow fairway sloping sharply to the left. If the drive has held this slender foothold another equally nail-biting shot follows down the hill to the new green, heavily bunkered on the left. So end 5,500 yards of considerable diversity and fascination, no less intriguing than a great many much longer courses.

*(MR)*

### Card of the course:

| | | | | | |
|---|---|---|---|---|---|
| 1. | 327 yards | par 4 | 10. | 383 yards | par 4 |
| 2. | 381 | 4 | 11. | 192 | 3 |
| 3. | 167 | 3 | 12. | 309 | 4 |
| 4. | 288 | 4 | 13. | 173 | 3 |
| 5. | 346 | 4 | 14. | 402 | 4 |
| 6. | 155 | 3 | 15. | 449 | 4 |
| 7. | 518 | 5 | 16. | 151 | 3 |
| 8. | 318 | 4 | 17. | 353 | 4 |
| 9. | 150 | 3 | 18. | 466 | 4 |
| Out: | 2650 yards | par 34 | | | |
| In: | 2878 yards | par 33 | | | |
| Total: | 5528 yards | par 67 | | s.s.s. 67 | |

# Moss Valley

*5080 yards; par 70*

$F$ull marks to Wrexham County Borough for providing a municipal golf course, a facility encountered all too rarely over the border in Cheshire and all too desperately needed. It was a brave move on Wrexham's part to create their course on such a hilly site. It is infinitely easier to construct and maintain a course on the flat, but what they have achieved is handsome in the extreme, both for its setting in an attractive valley and for its own lovely trees. It is worth all the exploration of minor roads and hilly villages necessary to find the course. By the time you have located it you will be a local!

The map shows the stream which affects several holes and informs play over the early part of the round. What the map does not show is the magnitude of the hills which are such a factor from the 5th. There is a hint of what is to come in the steep climb to the 2nd green laid out below a black-and-white house. To stand a realistic chance of pitching close the second shot will have to have been threaded accurately between the wooded hillside on the right and a copse on the left, the green otherwise hidden round behind trees.

**Moss Valley 3rd**

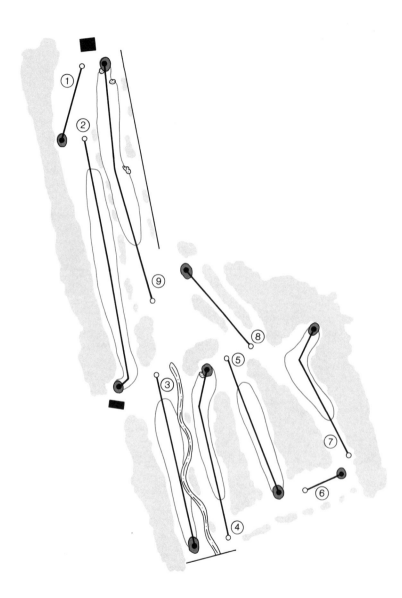

The climbing starts in earnest on the 5th, not a long par-4 as the crow flies but quite long enough when the second part of the fairway is such a steep incline. It is as nothing compared with the 85-yard ascent on the 6th. Happily both holes are blessed with glorious views and any misgivings one may have about the mountaineering are tempered by the splendid scenery.

The 7th starts the descent but it is a treacherous hole curving right, against the slope, the trees on both sides converging just behind the green. The view down the chute of trees to the 8th is another memorable one, particularly if your shot to it falls neither short nor into the trees on either side. The 9th is short as par-5s go, but the tee is low down and few will have the game to get up here in two.

*(MR)*

### Card of the course:

| | | |
|---|---|---|
| 1. | 150 yards | par 3 |
| 2. | 485 | 5 |
| 3. | 325 | 4 |
| 4. | 320 | 4 |
| 5. | 270 | 4 |
| 6. | 85 | 3 |
| 7. | 270 | 4 |
| 8. | 190 | 3 |
| 9. | 445 | 5 |
| Out: | 2540 yards | par 35 |
| Total: | 5080 yards | par 70 |

# Nefyn

*Old Course: 6342 yards; par 71; s.s.s. 71*

*New Course: 6548 yards; par 71; s.s.s. 71*

Throughout Great Britain there are many courses which can, with some justification, be described as Gardens of Eden. Right up at the top of the league, to be mentioned in the same breath as Cypress Point and Pebble Beach, is Nefyn. I am a habitual insomniac and had no difficulty in arriving on the 1st tee at 6.00 a.m. on a beautiful May morning. To have a spot such as this to oneself in the best light of day is one of life's richest pleasures. This part of the world is not particularly well-served with major roads but the journey to Nefyn is a must for any golfer simply to experience what has been described as "one of the most beautifully situated courses in Britain".

The idea to build a golf course here came in 1907 and by 1910 nine holes had been completed, with the full eighteen formally opened in 1913. The course may be a long way from any major centre of population but the pilgrimage to Nefyn has been made by many of the great names, such as James Braid and J.H. Taylor. In more recent years visitors have included Peter Alliss and Bernard Hunt and three of the finest golfers Wales has produced, Dai Rees, Dave Thomas and a past Masters winner, Ian Woosnam, who holds the course record of 67.

Recently eight further holes were added giving Nefyn a New Course, ten holes being shared between the Old and New. From their spectacular clifftop situation both courses enjoy wonderful views of the Irish Sea on every hole, located between the sandy beach of Porthdinllaen, the rugged cliffs of Borth Wen, and the mouth of the Afon Geich. The word "championship" is used far too freely, in my opinion, to describe golf courses unworthy of the title, but Nefyn certainly warrants it and many other accolades, too. Club members and visitors are fortunate indeed to have two courses from which to choose, though it comes as no surprise to find that the first time visitor is fairly certain to choose the Old

Course for it includes eight holes out on the famous peninsula. This may have a great deal to do with the golf and the breath-taking, spectacular situation, but may also have something to do with the watering hole, *The Ty Coch Inn* down on the beach close to the 12th green.

This was my first visit to Nefyn since the new holes have come into play, and as I have enjoyed the Old Course on numerous occasions I chose to play the New, though the first ten holes are common to both courses. The 1st is a most challenging downhill par-4 with a narrow and undulating fairway and a well-guarded green. Holes 2, 3 and 4 run perilously close to the cliffs and the most rigorous of these is the 4th, a thinking golfer's par-5. With a length of 477 yards it only just qualifies as a par-5 but well-positioned fairway bunkers and plenty of protection for the green bring course management to the fore. On this most recent visit the conditions could not have been calmer, the silence deafening, but what a different kettle of fish this is when the strong south-westerly winds beat in from the Irish Sea!

The medal tee of the short 5th is alarmingly close to the cliff edge and the hole deceives for length. I am sure underclubbing is common when visitors essay this hole for the first time. There was a touch of excitement to standing on the 6th tee, for the hole has been redesigned resulting in a much longer and more testing hole. It is slightly uphill and well-bunkered through the fairway. Then the 7th appears straightforward, with every yard of the fairway on view from tee to green, but so, too, is the gorse on the right in which a wild slice comes to grief. The 8th, a short, downhill par-4 with a right-to-left sloping fairway, is a little gem, a well-played tee shot leaving a downhill pitch to a brilliantly shielded green with no fewer than six bunkers. Having enjoyed a solitary round up to this point I had had plenty of opportunity to savour the wonderful setting and to appreciate the excellent condition of the course after such a cold and dry winter. It was appropriate that here I encountered the head greenkeeper and was able to congratulate him and his staff, especially as there are 26 holes to maintain.

As the halfway mark approaches there comes an uphill par-3 that forever plays longer than its suggested yardage. A well-played drive to the first hole on the back nine leaves a modest second shot to the under-protected green. It is here that the courses separate to go their own ways. The par-3 11th on the New Course, heralding the start of the unknown for me, plays away from the clubhouse and would appear quite insignificant at first glance but two cunningly placed traps, not quite greenside nor visible from the tee, can give rise to an awkward bunker shot. A relatively short par-4 comes next which is played from an elevated tee. Out-of-bounds flanks the left side and again well-positioned fairway bunkers await a drive which is only slightly off line on that side.

*Nefyn 14th green and 15th tee*

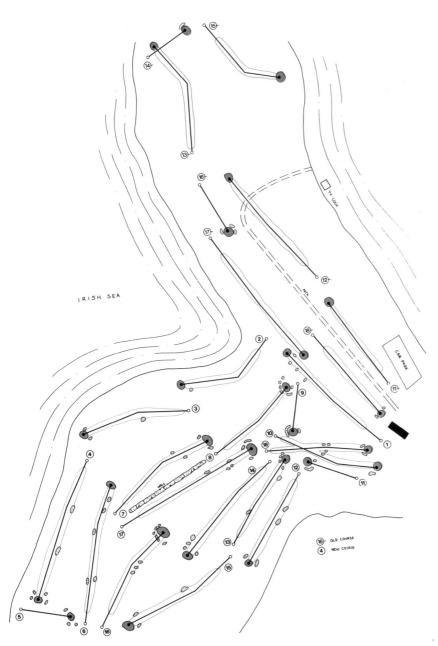

How grand it is to play a golf course of such high standard, with well thought-out bunkering, not only around the greens but also through the fairways! There is no great emphasis on length unlike so many modern designs. A fine example is the 13th, a slight dog-leg right with its posse of bunkers short of and around the green, calling for accuracy both from the tee and on the approach shot. It is followed by a longer par-4 with no great peril from the tee in the way of bunkers or savage rough but woe betide if you play a weak and erratic shot to the green!

With just four holes to play on the New Course the next one is nothing short of an absolute snorter. From the low-lying white tee there are two options but how daunting the bolder route appears to be with the boundary fence running the length of the hole from tee to green! Playing safe lengthens the hole by taking a line right of a perfectly positioned fairway bunker. Even the heartiest of hits for the second shot may well run out of steam before the putting surface. The hole has no greenside bunkers, but it does have a couple of very astutely placed traps 55 and 35 yards short of the green, and every golfer knows how difficult a bunker shot of that length can be. Having just played the frightening 15th, a teaser of a dog-leg right comes next with its eight bunkers to contend with, three on the right of the fairway and five around the green.

The longest of the par-5s on either course is the 17th on the New Course. The tee shot, played slightly downhill, needs only to avoid two big grassy mounds to the right of the fairway but it all starts to happen for the long second shot. Further well-placed fairway bunkers give cause for concern and tacking in from the right seems the more favourable option, while any wayward approach shot to the left of the green is likely to find either of two hefty bunkers. How well all these greens were playing despite a late and cold spring!

The steepest climb on the course is not during play of a hole but comes between the 17th green and 18th tee. From this fine vantage point a lapse in concentration can be forgiven as the view over the Irish Sea is taken in once again. It was like a mill pond on the morning of my visit while in the opposite, landward direction the ever-present, magnificent Snowdonia Range dominated the scene in its towering glory. The play on the final hole of the New Course is across the 10th fairway, heading back towards the clubhouse. The fairway is undulating in its early stages but if the drive is well-planned all that remains is a kind and straightforward approach shot.

If you think that with three hours of play completed on eighteen glorious golf holes you could put your clubs in the car boot and drive away, stand on the 11th tee of the Old Course and see if you can resist the temptation before you. The 11th and 12th run over tumbling fairways parallel to the beach and the beautiful seaside hamlet of Porthdinllaen, its appeal such that it is preserved by the National Trust. It is at this point that many a thirsty player drops down the little path to *Ty Coch* before returning to the serious matter of golf. The pulpit 14th tee is a grand spot, too, overlooking a fine hole to a low-lying green and the bay and mountains beyond, while the 15th tee is the perfect vantage point from which to watch the seals frolicking in the bay below your feet.

Homeward bound the 17th is a testing par-5 with rough and a roadway to the left, the cliffs dropping straight down to the sea on the right. I have no doubt a great many promising scorecards have been ruined on this hole. The Old Course ends with a short par-4 with few frustrations, but perhaps that is how golf should end in the Garden of Eden. Nefyn is the sort of course to which, once played, the visitor will want to return again and again.

*(PL)*

## Card of the course (Old Course):

| | | | | | |
|---|---|---|---|---|---|
| 1. | 458 yards | par 4 | 10. | 415 yards | par 4 |
| 2. | 374 | 4 | 11. | 323 | 4 |
| 3. | 397 | 4 | 12. | 478 | 5 |
| 4. | 477 | 5 | 13. | 415 | 4 |
| 5. | 156 | 3 | 14. | 165 | 3 |
| 6. | 442 | 4 | 15. | 328 | 4 |
| 7. | 401 | 4 | 16. | 188 | 3 |
| 8. | 327 | 4 | 17. | 505 | 5 |
| 9. | 166 | 3 | 18. | 327 | 4 |
| Out: | 3198 yards | par 35 | | | |
| In: | 3144 yards | par 36 | | | |
| Total: | 6342 yards | par 71 | | s.s.s. 71 | |

## Card of the course (New Course):

| | | | | | |
|---|---|---|---|---|---|
| 1. | 458 yards | par 4 | 10. | 415 yards | par 4 |
| 2. | 374 | 4 | 11. | 181 | 3 |
| 3. | 397 | 4 | 12. | 349 | 4 |
| 4. | 477 | 5 | 13. | 344 | 4 |
| 5. | 156 | 3 | 14. | 401 | 4 |
| 6. | 442 | 4 | 15. | 405 | 4 |
| 7. | 401 | 4 | 16. | 367 | 4 |
| 8. | 327 | 4 | 17. | 512 | 5 |
| 9. | 166 | 3 | 18. | 376 | 4 |
| Out: | 3198 yards | par 35 | | | |
| In: | 3350 yards | par 36 | | | |
| Total: | 6548 yards | par 71 | | s.s.s. 71 | |

# North Wales

*6247 yards; par 71; s.s.s. 71*

This golf course, highly acclaimed by the likes of the great Henry Cotton who called it a gem back in the 1950s, was summed up by the golfing scribe, G.A. Philpot: "How can I describe the almost incomparable setting of this course?" It is surely something to be experienced rather than written about, a most beautiful setting of sea, land and mountain. Similar views can, of course, be savoured

from neighbouring Maesdu divided from North Wales only by the little railway which has carried millions of tourists to the queen of resorts, Llandudno, over the last 150 years. What an opportunity for the visiting golfer having a traditional championship links in North Wales and a parkland course of equal status, Maesdu, separated only by the width of a railway track!

**North Wales 16th**

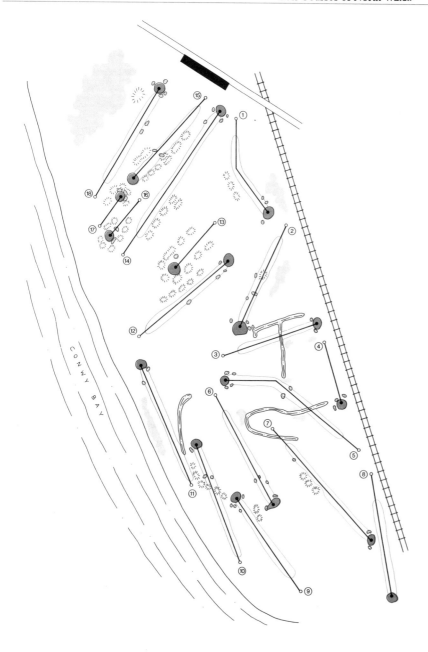

The club's founder, one Mr. Tancred Disraeli Cummins, was ably assisted by Harold Hilton of the Royal Liverpool Golf Club, winner of the 32nd Open Championship at Muirfield back in 1892 and again five years later at his home club. Golfers from Royal Liverpool had a tremendous influence in establishing the game along this stretch of the North Wales coast and Hilton's influence at the North Wales Club was not at all in his declining years but during that golden period between winning his first and second Opens!

My visit to the course, although having played it on numerous previous occasions, was purely to familiarise myself with recent changes to the layout. What a morning I chose on a bleak January day! The usual south-westerly wind was replaced by a bitterly cold easterly. The opening tee shot on this dog-leg left is a shot-maker's delight as a controlled draw or fade is required depending on which side of the ball one stands. For the player thinking more of safety a long iron is more the order of the day. Emphasis on position is essential on the next hole because of a curtain of gorse down the left side and a niggly grassy mound stretching some 60 yards along the left centre of the fairway. Although this is not a very long par-4, played into the prevailing wind it can prove very costly.

Each hole on the links has its own name, the 3rd called *The Collins* after that brilliant duo Fred Collins (the club's very first professional from 1894 to 1938) and his nephew, Sid (professional from 1938 to 1979). Both were winners of the Welsh Professional Championship and highly respected teachers of the game. The railway line stretches the full length of, and perilously close to, the first of the course's par-3 holes. Should you think you are home and dry with a well-placed tee shot to the green think again! The tricky two-tier putting surface so easily takes its toll. It is followed by *The Hill*, a par-5 with a water hazard to its left and the hill after which the hole is named coming into play in the later stages of the hole to a well-trapped green.

Then a run of three holes takes us to the furthest point of the course: the 6th a fairly straightforward par-4 and the 7th having a slightly undulating fairway and, once again, the railway to contend with. Having not played the course for the last two years I was very much looking forward to playing the recently redesigned 8th which I had heard so much about and it certainly lived up to expectation. One is faced with a blind tee shot, but that is how it always has been to my recollection, on what I would call a beautifully old-fashioned golf hole with its humps and hollows and narrow fairway. The relocated two-tier green demands accuracy and judgement of distance of the highest calibre.

The 9th is the first of three par-4s running more or less parallel with the sea shore. Although fairly short in distance an abundance of trouble awaits a wayward drive left and a number of bunkers positioned close to the front of the green will swallow any weak approach shot. Then the first of the homeward nine, named *The Ruins*, features another blind drive and a pair of extremely well-positioned fairway cross-bunkers some 40 yards short of the green and calls for two fine shots, the second of which needs to be played on a line slightly left of the low-lying green.

As I stood on the 11th tee even on this bitingly cold winter morning the backdrop of the Great Orme and the Conwy Mountains captivated my attention. This hole with the sea shore to its left, water hazards to the right and running slightly uphill fully justifies being Stroke Index 1. What protection from the elements there is is merely a high grass mound to the left of the green. Having been presented with another blind tee shot on the 12th at least a generously wide fairway awaits. There are certainly no awards for playing up short with the second shot as, again, a number of well-positioned traps lie in wait. The well-designed and undulating green requires a dextrous stroke.

As I walked to the 13th tee with only the hardiest of golfers in sight it was never the less easy to see why numerous championships have been staged here including the 1995 Welsh Amateur Team event. *Hades*, the 13th, seen by many as one of golf's finest short holes, is again what I would call a grand old fashioned design,

played from a pulpit tee to a flat green which is encircled by hillocks. Club selection can vary from a long iron to a driver when challenging the dominant south-westerly wind. The last and longest of the par-5s is next.

The 15th tee is adjacent to the clubhouse and requires a well-planned first shot as there are two cunningly placed bunkers situated at the entrance to the valley where the fairway is constricted. A long, narrow, sloping green awaits an accurate second shot. I am sure that most golfers who have played North Wales will have holes 16 and 17 logged in their minds for years on end. The 16th was christened *O.L.* after the expletives that are often heard when golfers first arrive on the tee with nothing in front of them but a sea of wilderness and only the top of the flag just visible 150 yards away. Nothing will avoid the sandhills, dunes and hidden bunkers other than a precision shot.

In contrast on the 17th (the *L.O.* hole named after two golfers who on first sight said, " 'Ello, what do we 'ave 'ere?") I am sure there have been many hole-in-one celebrations and, conversely, a profusion of high scores. It is that sort of hole. The final hole, with the tee shot played from amongst the gorse bushes, has out-of-bounds to its left and any drive leaking out right will be followed by an awkward second shot to a well-protected green and, again, out-of-bounds only a few yards beyond.

*(PL)*

| Card of the course: | | | | | |
|---|---|---|---|---|---|
| 1. | 344 yards | par 4 | 10. | 400 yards | par 4 |
| 2. | 359 | 4 | 11. | 420 | 4 |
| 3. | 338 | 4 | 12. | 359 | 4 |
| 4. | 200 | 3 | 13. | 182 | 3 |
| 5. | 510 | 5 | 14. | 530 | 5 |
| 6. | 385 | 4 | 15. | 334 | 4 |
| 7. | 498 | 5 | 16. | 151 | 3 |
| 8. | 387 | 4 | 17. | 120 | 3 |
| 9. | 347 | 4 | 18. | 383 | 4 |
| Out: | 3368 yards | par 37 | | | |
| In: | 2879 yards | par 34 | | | |
| Total: | 6247 yards | par 71 | | s.s.s. 71 | |

# Northop Country Park

*6735 yards; par 72; s.s.s. 73*

Northop is unique as far as golf in North Wales is concerned. It is the only major development in what you might call "the English style": in other words it is part of a major complex involving a connection with the St. David's Park Hotel, with luxury housing within the course itself, possessing its own conference and enter-

tainment facilities, and balancing corporate and society golf with the needs of its own membership. Through its parent company it is now linked with Carden Park, a few miles distant south of Chester, the glories of which are described in *Golf Courses of Cheshire (Sigma Leisure)*. Observing a group of businessmen

**Northop 16th**

gathered round their flip-charts in one of the conference rooms I could not help trying to devise all sorts of management training games involving the course itself as I drove home afterwards!

John Jacobs is credited with the design (his impressive biography can be found at the back of the book) and given his pedigree as both a player and designer you would expect something formidable. What he has produced here is actually rather gentle. Never as you stand on the tee (whatever your level of competence) do you freeze, terrified at the prospect before you, as you might at any number of contemporary courses elsewhere. You are not required compulsorily to make a heroic carry either from tee or to green. The greens are mildly undulating, hardly punishing in the Augusta manner, and almost invariably open at the front. What you have to do, though, is approach the green at the right angle and at the correct strength or the subtle shaping of the ground will almost certainly throw the ball off into one of Jacobs's deep and cunningly shaped bunkers. Escape from these requires a deft touch (or impressive technique if you find yourself in the back of one of these bunkers with the sand sloping downhill away from you). In other words, Jacobs has made it possible for most of us to get round relatively unimpeded, knowing that we will make our own trouble largely through our incompetence. The scratch golfer seeks different challenges and these are here, too, particularly when play is from the back tees and the pins are in the tight positions possible on many of these greens. The greens, incidentally, are built to a USGA specification and can be made to play very fast indeed. The course may be young (opening in June 1994) but it has already played host to the Welsh PGA National Championship.

The medal tees give a course of 6,735 yards, with only three par-4s over 400-yards in length, and there are many teeing sites on each hole, offering variety to the member and flexibility to the greenkeeper who must regulate wear and tear. These teeing grounds are often in free forms, thankfully ridding us of the curse of the 100-yard strip tee. Probably a course of more than 7,000 yards could have been forced into the space, but Jacobs's restraint has ensured that there is nothing cramped and that play on one hole is unlikely to interfere with play on any other. On some holes the difference between white and yellow plates is considerable and, as the 1st hole beats an uphill path, I should not complain about utilising the yellow tees here. We might drive the bunkers on either side but, more likely, we will be troubled at the prospect of disturbing the peace of the houses up the right with a mild slice.

Such is progress to the green. The 2nd is a question of correct clubbing, not only to avoid the many bunkers but also to find the right part of a big green.

Stroke 1 comes on the 3rd, a hole with more guile than outright devilment. True, you can go out-of-bounds on the left or clatter into trees on the right, but the real skill is in avoiding either of the ditches which pinch the drive and then not being deceived by the ridge between the bunkers which is actually some way in front of the green, though it appears otherwise. The downhill 4th, on the other hand, is asking to be driven. A line over the right-hand bunker sets up a feasible approach from one of the forward tees, but the further back you go (and you can go back 100 yards here) the more problematic the carry and the greater the possibility of dying a death in the trees on the right. The 5th, too, is almost 70 yards shorter from the women's tee than from the back of the medal tee. Whatever the actual length played, it is necessary to add a club or two to climb the slight hill to the 3-level green.

On a first acquaintance it is not obvious why the 6th should be Stroke 3, though big hitters might be tempted to cut a little off the corner and find trees or an out-of-bounds fence on the right. The 7th, on the other hand, is quite a villain, slightly altered since the advent of houses to the right. None of us wishes to enter their gardens uninvited, nor to visit the ponds recently added down the right. In aiming safely to the left we bring a big tree into play. You can go either side of it, but many of us will try to go over it (or through it). The professionals might expect to have to squeeze their drives between that tree and the houses on the right. Theirs is a different game and Jacobs has catered for it.

All of us will fancy our chances on the 8th, a downhill par-5. It is also, for the present, the prettiest hole, curling to the right through an avenue of trees. A well-placed bunker on the right will force long-hitters out to the left and some of them may perish in the lily pond on that side. Even if the green is within range, the angle of the putting surface is such that the shot must be shaped around the bunkers, shots that were nearly good enough perishing in the undulations just in front of the green. To bring play back to the club-house the 9th bears sharply left in a dog-leg, the slope of the ground helping all feeble shots into the bunkers on the left of both the fairway and the green.

The back nine is somewhat shorter and the 10th might most readily be described as a mirror image of the 10th at The Belfry. Some will drive this green, over the stream and trees on the left,

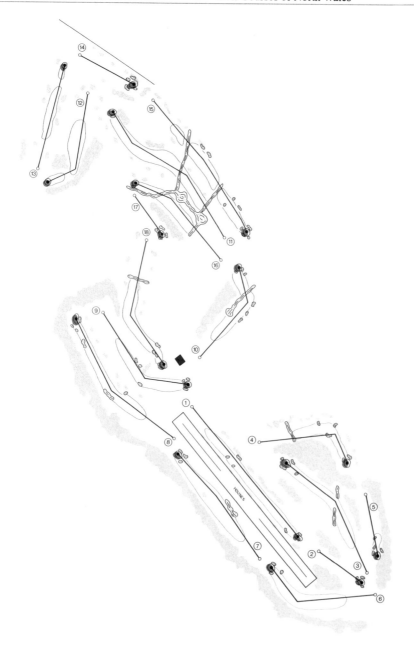

others will find the right-hand bunkers in playing safe away from the stream. Those of us who lay up short might just find we have no shot over the trees to the green. It is not a long hole, but we have to elect the correct strategy and execute it perfectly. Then, on the 11th, the obvious hazards are the two ditches which must be cleared and the ponds to the left of the fairway. However, the hole's name, *Wooden Heartache*, hints at the serious problem for golfers of all standards posed by no more than a handful of trees around which the fairway bends over the final 200 yards. Good golf architecture does not necessarily involve the moving of thousands of tons of earth.

The 12th, too, is all about position, the drive needing to flirt with out-of-bounds on the left if the pitch is not to be blocked out by more trees. This is parkland golf at its simplest and best, and handsome with it. From the tee the 13th seems utterly simple, but from the forward tees it is all too easy to find a wicked lie in the links-like undulations which cross the fairway just short of the green, raised up in front of the elegant parish church. The short 14th plays along the road in front of the church, a matter of noting the correct distance from the tee in use with the back tee 60 yards behind the women's.

At Northop the par-5s are, unusually, amongst the higher stroke ratings and the 15th is a fine example of the architect's using simple means to sort out the Category 1 players from the rest. We, the rest, are happy enough if neither our first nor second shot expires in the ditches which cross the fairway. Real players have to land their drives in the narrow part of the fairway as it bears right with bunkers on the left and moundwork on the right. In the prevailing wind they will expect to get on in two. In contrast, the 16th is all about position for everyone. Two ponds and a ditch on the right dominate play and the pitch is made over another stretch of water, with a rascal of a holly bush on the right of the green to thwart those who aim away from the water.

Most of us will already have won or lost by the 17th, so it is fair that the short 17th comes as the final stroke hole, the green generous for a hole so short, though it is possible to position the pin very close to one or other of the bunkers. Some idea of the difference in golf between the tiger and the average player is indicated by the substantial variance in the last hole as played from white or yellow tees. From the front it is not too hard to pierce the gap between the trees to find the fairway where it turns to the left.

Try it from 30 yards further back! It is essential to find that part of the fairway if there is to be a realistic long shot in to the green behind the club-house.

*(MR)*

### Card of the course:

| | | | | | |
|---|---|---|---|---|---|
| 1. | 541 yards | par 5 | 10. | 354 yards | par 4 |
| 2. | 180 | 3 | 11. | 559 | 5 |
| 3. | 441 | 4 | 12. | 349 | 4 |
| 4. | 355 | 4 | 13. | 349 | 4 |
| 5. | 203 | 3 | 14. | 192 | 3 |
| 6. | 393 | 4 | 15. | 522 | 5 |
| 7. | 428 | 4 | 16. | 378 | 4 |
| 8. | 505 | 5 | 17. | 156 | 3 |
| 9. | 390 | 4 | 18. | 440 | 4 |
| Out: | 3436 yards | par 36 | | | |
| In: | 3299 yards | par 36 | | | |
| Total: | 6735 yards | par 72 | | s.s.s. 73 | |

# Old Colwyn

*5243 yards; par 68; s.s.s. 66*

Old Colwyn is enjoyable holiday golf and a charming antidote to the rigours of the several fine links courses in the area. Indeed I played it on holiday many years ago with my father and indelibly printed on my mind is the vision of unloading my golf bag from the boot of the car, a number of balls falling out of an unzipped pocket and racing away down the hill — all the way to sea, for all I know. The clubhouse, obviously, sits on top of a hill above Old Colwyn giving tremendous views not only of the sweep of the bay but also of the enveloping hills.

Put your modest green fee in the "Trust the Golfer" box on a weekday and you may have the course almost to yourself but in North Wales it will not be many holes before you are invited to join

**Old Colwyn 2nd**

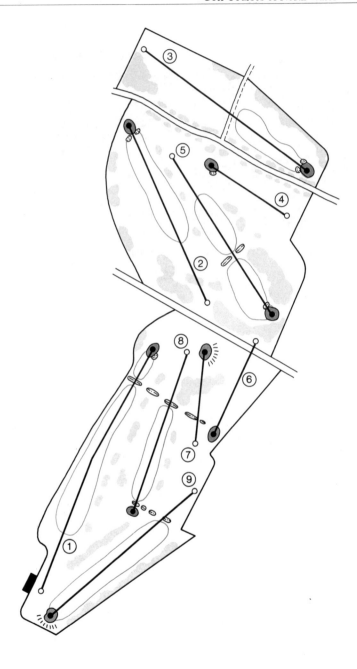

a match in progress and the members' wisdom and experience may save the odd silly club selection (always tricky on a hilly site). Even if you are on your own here you will only have to play truly blind to a green if your golf has been such that you deserve it! It is more likely that you will relish the chance of pulling all the stops out in several attempts to drive the greens on downhill par-4 holes.

The opening hole is stringent enough with an out-of-bounds fence on the left, the side you would prefer to be given the cross-slope on the fairway. Most drives finish in the bottom of a valley after which it is necessary to decide whether or not the second shot can clear a shallow ditch a little way short of the green. All the greens are wired to keep off the sheep which roam the course. The sheep, however, ensure nicely cropped fairways (and decent fertilisation, too).

Over the road, the 2nd plays longer than the card suggests as it climbs steadily. Then a country walk through umpteen gates leads to whichever of the many tees scattered about the hillside you are required to play from on the 3rd/12th. The views are impressive and the prospect of driving uplifting. Attempt to drive the green if you wish, but as you approach it the road on the right appears to close in as does the out-of-bounds trouble so abundant on the left.

The short 4th ought not to inconvenience us before launching out over the trees on the downhill 5th, able to be driven in theory. All too frequently we clatter into more trees on the left and the approach from that side is not easy with a devilishly contrived bunker eating into the green. Over the road (*literally* from one of the tees) the 6th is simple enough, but before leaving for the green take a look to the right to see what lies in store on the next hole. This challenging par-3 is not long but you must hit the ball high over a line of trees, taking ample club also to allow for the climb to the plateau green.

If you take account of the slopes on the 8th you might fancy your chances on a pot-shot at the green, but there is a little ditch on the left front and the putting surface is of no great area and cut as a ledge into the slope. The round concludes with a lovely hole, albeit grinding uphill, but the green, the only flat ground on a pinnacle, gives views which make the climb thoroughly worthwhile. Variety is added to an 18-hole round by quite separate tees on most holes and surely vanity will compel us to go for those enticing drives next time round!

*(MR)*

### Card of the course:

| | | | | | |
|---|---|---|---|---|---|
| 1. | 476 yards | par 5 | 10. | 476 yards | par 5 |
| 2. | 349 | 4 | 11. | 342 | 4 |
| 3. | 372 | 4 | 12. | 371 | 4 |
| 4. | 146 | 3 | 13. | 168 | 3 |
| 5. | 342 | 4 | 14. | 302 | 4 |
| 6. | 183 | 3 | 15. | 149 | 3 |
| 7. | 164 | 3 | 16. | 151 | 3 |
| 8. | 287 | 4 | 17. | 300 | 4 |
| 9. | 339 | 4 | 18. | 326 | 4 |

| | | | |
|---|---|---|---|
| Out: | 2658 yards | par 34 | |
| In: | 2585 yards | par 34 | |
| Total: | 5243 yards | par 68 | s.s.s. 66 |

# Old Padeswood

*6685 yards; par 72; s.s.s. 72*

$I$t is more the job of the local historian than the itinerant golfer to try to untangle the web of intrigue which led to the existence of two entirely separate golf clubs side by side in the Alyn Valley between Mold and Chester. No doubt the members of each club will loyally defend the superiority of their club over its neighbour. It is the happy lot of *this* itinerant golfer not to have to make any

choice. I was lucky enough to play them on consecutive days and to be able to enjoy their similarities and differences with equanimity.

Old Padeswood (despite its name) is the more recent club, founded in 1977, and it occupies part of the land once occupied by Padeswood and Buckley, so *you* will begin to appreciate that

**Old Padeswood 4th**

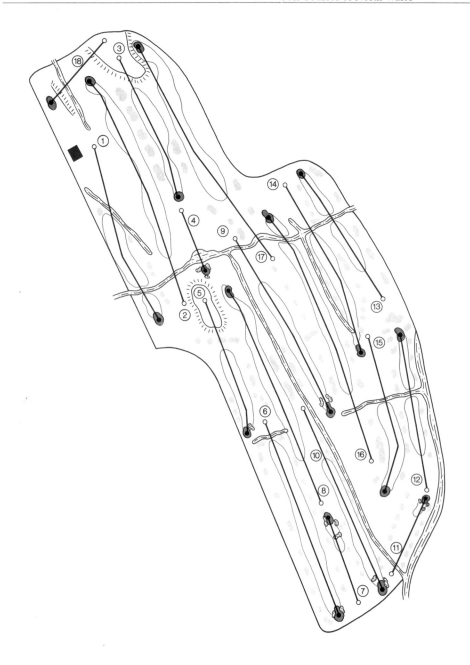

Machiavelli had a hand in events here and *I* begin to see why the reasons for the courses' similarities are more than just geography. Old Padeswood is considerably longer and both hillier and flatter. This seemingly contradictory statement is accounted for by the fact that the holes in the area close to the clubhouse enjoy the benefits of some seriously undulating ground while the rest of the course is laid out on traditionally flat meadowland.

The 1st is a decidedly difficult start with a drive over a stream, a mound on the right and out-of-bounds left. There is no chickening out here, nor is there on the second shot, blind over a big mound to a raised green too close to the fence on the right for comfort. The first time visitor is unlikely to repair the damage to his card on the 2nd, either. The drive may be simple enough but the next shot must be kept to the right of a marker post as it is played blind over a ridge. Veer to the left and you will find your pitch shot blocked out by a second and much steeper mound. This green is not one to overshoot with a tidy drop beyond.

The course planner suggests that the tee shot on the 3rd should be placed centre left of the fairway. It takes good golf to achieve that with trees and out-of-bounds on the right and a big drop to the 17th fairway on the left. Because the tee is much higher than the fairway any directional inaccuracy seems to be magnified. Even a strong hit may give no sight of the green down the hill under the marker post in the centre of the ridge.

Suddenly we have forsaken the ocean swell for a hole on the level, the short 4th, and it is worth bringing the camera for this hole alone. A ditch has been enlarged and dammed to form an attractive lake directly in front of the green. Bunkers on either side and a steep hill through the back complete a striking setting. If the hole is cut close to the ridge on this two-level green putting may be more than testing. The next tee is on the very top of the hill behind.

From the 5th tee it is inadvisable to aim directly at the green: the huge slope on the ground in the landing zone will send the ball tearing off towards the out-of-bounds on the right. Locals know exactly which distant tree to aim at and then the pitch is not too demanding. And that, for quite some time, is the end of the rough-and-tumble, with only a little ridge on the 8th to relieve the flatness until the roller coaster golf of the finish. That is not to say that scoring will necessarily be any easier with length in plenty on many holes, not least the 6th which, interestingly, is 25 yards longer from the women's red tee than it is from the men's yellow one, though the women are allowed an extra stroke here.

Only long, straight hitting will suffice from here until the relative peace of the 11th, ditches punishing on at least one side of most fairways. Length, however, is not always an advantage. From the 12th tee the most obvious hazard is the river running behind a prominent bank on the right, but unless you choose the right club you may perish in the less visible ditch crossing the fairway. The green is narrow between trees. The 13th is not dissimilar with another ditch crossing at about the 250 yard mark. While few of us would threaten it from the very back, that ditch poses a real threat to most of us from the more forward tees.

The 14th is a fine strategic hole made all the harder by an internal out-of-bounds down the right. The fairway drifts that way and the entrance to the green is very narrow with a ditch closing in almost to the very front right of the putting surface. A sharp dog-leg leads to the hugely long par-5 16th. It would be an unremarkable hole were it not for the ditch which crosses the fairway where most of us would prefer it did not. So we are forced to lay up short of it with our second shots and hit a short to medium iron in to the green.

The second successive par-5, the 17th, returns to the heavily undulating ground encountered at the beginning of the round. A decently long drive may open up the possibility of reaching the green in two but most of us, most of the time, must settle for a blind second shot over a marker post into a sunken valley from which the pitch is played high over another ridge and steeply down the other side to a complicatedly contoured green. Here we are right under the car park of neighbouring Padeswood and Buckley and, as it happens, both courses close with a short hole, Old Padeswood's quite a tester with perfect club selection needed to ensure that the ball will not drop short as it crosses a river valley. Overclub, however, and you may be faced with a ticklish downhill pitch, the green always running away from you.

*(MR)*

| Card of the course: | | | | | |
|---|---|---|---|---|---|
| 1. | 413 yards | par 4 | 10. | 445 yards | par 4 |
| 2. | 532 | 5 | 11. | 174 | 3 |
| 3. | 335 | 4 | 12. | 346 | 4 |
| 4. | 142 | 3 | 13. | 323 | 4 |
| 5. | 305 | 4 | 14. | 416 | 4 |
| 6. | 455 | 4 | 15. | 356 | 4 |
| 7. | 205 | 3 | 16. | 584 | 5 |
| 8. | 503 | 5 | 17. | 510 | 5 |
| 9. | 446 | 4 | 18. | 195 | 3 |
| Out: | 3336 yards | par 36 | | | |
| In: | 3349 yards | par 36 | | | |
| Total: | 6685 yards | par 72 | | s.s.s. 72 | |

# Padeswood and Buckley

*5982 yards; par 70; s.s.s. 69*

One of those quirks of fate decrees that not only should Padeswood and Buckley and Old Padeswood share a boundary fence and a little ancestry but, strange to tell, they follow back to back in this book. They make a good foil for each other and the visitor with sufficient time to spare could do worse than play both courses, though in which order I cannot say. Padeswood and Buckley is the senior of the two clubs, though their courses are of similar age, and this one is by some 700 yards the shorter. It does not undulate as violently as Old Padeswood does around the clubhouse, but neither is it ever as flat as Old Padeswood's lengthy meadowland stretch. Moreover Padeswood and Buckley enjoys the benefits of a more generous allocation of trees throughout the round.

Padeswood's 1st is one of only two par-4s over 400 yards long and at any other stage of the round would not be thought too demanding. At the start of the round most of us will be happy neither to crash into the clubhouse on the right nor scuff our tee shot into the hedge on the left. The green has a narrow entrance between bunkers. As par-3s go the 2nd is quite long and distinctly treacherous with out-of-bounds very close on the left. In early October this green was littered with crabs newly fallen from one of the trees on the left, the scent of embryonic cider in the air. What was it Walter Hagen said about not forgetting to smell the flowers along the way?

After a dog-leg made just that bit trickier with the ground falling towards the green comes *Coppa*, the first of a pair of

**Padeswood and Buckley 14th**

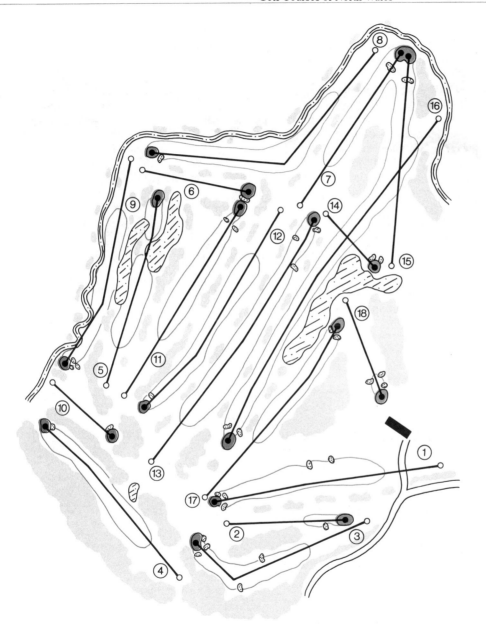

new holes. It is very narrow between the trees though the mighty should be able to drive clear of the worst trouble. With wooded hills beyond and a stream in the bottom of the valley this is a delightful part of the course.

Before you play the 5th for the first time climb the ladder by the tee, not only to admire the view but also to take in the strategy of the hole. It would be folly to drive blindly so far with a helpful wind that the ball sinks into the lake splitting the fairway in front. Equally you would prefer not to have to play your second shot across the lake from a hanging lie. Whatever the golfing outcome you are likely to warm to the beauty of the hole, particularly as it was for me with the sun sparkling on the rippled surface and a swan gliding imperiously from one side to the other.

You make your own difficulties on the 6th and 7th, nor should the 8th trouble you as long as you keep out of the river running in a long curve all the way down the right. It is the sort of dog-leg that encourages golfers of all ability to cut the corner and try to reach the green in two. You would welcome a shot or two in hand here before you tackle the 9th, *Alyn Bank*. The name is not inappropriate: the river meanders in and out of the fairway on the right. You cannot duck the challenge for trees and further water on the left dispose of that possibility. Even after a straight drive the approach shot is not for the timid with the river making its last incursion only just in front of the green and three bunkers set in the upslope to the left of the putting surface.

After the new 10th play runs back and forth over the more open central higher ground until the gentle drop shot to the 14th green. It is rarely more than a wedge but the presence of a lake on the right can be enough to force us into one or other bunker on the left. Like the 7th, with which it shares a green, the 15th is a drive and pitch hole separated from Old Padeswood only by the stream. The hole names here are for the most part descriptive, some in English others in Welsh – a happy practice. Cryptically the 7th is called *LL* and the 15th *RR*.

Then it is time for some substantial hitting on the seriously long par-5 16th. The drive easily perishes in the lake on the left, a nature sanctuary. So too might the second shot plunge in, while the pitch must be made to the correct part of a stepped green. The 17th runs down the other side of the lake, an inviting hole, before you are asked to choose your club carefully to hit uphill on the not so short par-3 18th, *Caia*. Up here you look down on those putting the 17th

green at Old Padeswood. You have finished. They still have a testing par-3 to delay their progress to the bar.

*(MR)*

| Card of the course: | | | | | |
|---|---|---|---|---|---|
| 1. | 405 yards | par 4 | 10. | 146 yards | par 3 |
| 2. | 213 | 3 | 11. | 358 | 4 |
| 3. | 345 | 4 | 12. | 422 | 4 |
| 4. | 323 | 4 | 13. | 503 | 5 |
| 5. | 332 | 4 | 14. | 128 | 3 |
| 6. | 196 | 3 | 15. | 349 | 4 |
| 7. | 312 | 4 | 16. | 562 | 5 |
| 8. | 478 | 5 | 17. | 372 | 4 |
| 9. | 363 | 4 | 18. | 175 | 3 |
| Out: | 2967 yards | par 35 | | | |
| In: | 3015 yards | par 35 | | | |
| Total: | 5982 yards | par 70 | | s.s.s. 69 | |

# Penmaenmawr

*5350 yards; par 67; s.s.s. 66*

The Penmaenmawr Golf Club was founded back in 1910 and officially opened by Col. C.H. Derbishire, the first club captain. This delightful 9-hole course with its warm and friendly welcome is situated at the foot of the Moel Llys Mountains. Before start of play savour the view of the Sychnant Pass, the Great Orme and the Conwy estuary.

The par-4 1st is downhill, a relatively easy tee shot. The line is down the left-hand side of the fairway because of a solitary tree on the right. Size up the pitch with caution: out of bounds lies directly behind the green. The next hole, short though you may think it for a par-4, has its difficulties. Trees to your right and one of several

**Penmaenmawr 9th**

105

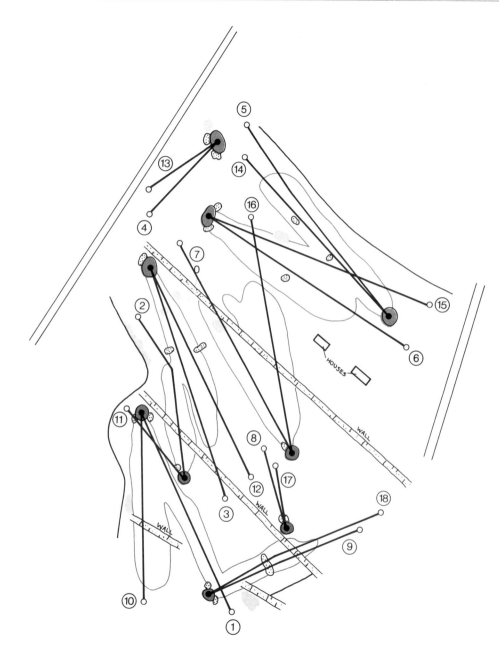

dry stone walls run parallel with the fairway. A bold pitch to a plateau green pays dividends.

A short climb to the 3rd tee sets you up to open your shoulders for the drive. The downhill approach to the fast running green has its pitfalls if you are off line or too bold. The first of the par-3s comes next with its recently relocated green and undulating approach. An errant shot to the left is a card-wrecker.

A challenging uphill 365-yard slight dog-leg, the 5th, is out on the far side of the course and provides a true examination of the golfer's accuracy and ability to judge distance. Out-of-bounds flanks the left side from tee to green. Whatever club you have in your hands for the stroke to the plateau green, may I recommend you put it back in your bag and take one two-clubs stronger? The embankment at the back will return your ball safely to the putting surface. The following hole, with its tee at the highest point and the Alttwen Mountains and Conwy estuary in the distance, demands an accurate tee shot. A posse of tall trees to the right of the fairway waits to arrest the wayward shot. The green, protected by two bunkers, slopes seaward – as do the majority.

Heading homewards now, the 7th with a stone wall running not quite parallel to the fairway plays every inch of the allocated 378 yards. A well-placed greenside bunker, probably the toughest on the course, will swallow up a weak shot and the two-tier green calls for a keen eye and deft touch. The uphill par-3 8th, with another wall within sniffing distance of the right edge of the green and gorse bushes beyond, requires an accurate carry favouring the left side.

An out-of-bounds to the left of a left-to-right sloping fairway makes the drive from the elevated 9th tee somewhat daunting. A bunker slap-bang in the middle of the fairway can punish the average golfer's best strike and the well-protected last green calls for a precise second shot. The second nine holes are played from alternative tees to the same greens which makes for considerable variation and much new thinking.

*(PL)*

### Card of the course:

| | | | | | |
|---|---|---|---|---|---|
| 1. | 379 yards | par 4 | 10. | 346 yards | par 4 |
| 2. | 277 | 4 | 11. | 149 | 3 |
| 3. | 369 | 4 | 12. | 375 | 4 |
| 4. | 158 | 3 | 13. | 147 | 3 |
| 5. | 365 | 4 | 14. | 361 | 4 |
| 6. | 396 | 4 | 15. | 398 | 4 |
| 7. | 378 | 4 | 16. | 361 | 4 |
| 8. | 135 | 3 | 17. | 104 | 3 |
| 9. | 298 | 4 | 18. | 354 | 4 |

| | | |
|---|---|---|
| Out: | 2755 yards | par 34 |
| In: | 2595 yards | par 33 |
| Total: | 5350 yards | par 67 — s.s.s. 66 |

# Penycae

*4176 yards; par 64; s.s.s. 65*

One night at the end of August 1940 German bombers mounted a spectacular air raid on Ruabon Mountain up above Penycae setting it alight with incendiary bombs. They did the very same thing on the following night this time with high explosives. The Germans thought they had bombed Liverpool having flown up a radar beam from France and, at a point at which that beam intersected with another, they dropped their bombs. The RAF discovered their tactics and succeeded in bending the beam. Until recently I discovered the little golf course this was all I knew about Penycae.

It could have been very unfair to Penycae that I visited it just after playing in rapid succession the world class courses at Royal

**Penycae 8th**

Troon and Royal Dornoch in Scotland and Kennemer in Holland, yet it accounted for itself admirably. Of course there is no comparison, for Penycae is a short, almost executive length, 9-hole layout of very recent provenance but there is as much character in the 2nd, 3rd and 8th holes as on many another 18-hole circuit. The club is young and vigorous and there are plans to expand to 18 holes in time.

That 2nd is an exceedingly unforgiving hole with the narrowest of gaps in the trees giving a tiny glimpse of the flag some 200 yards away. If anything it plays uphill so it really is a full length par-3 and with out-of-bounds on the right and, interestingly, a bunker at the back of the green there is no alternative to hitting and holding.

The 3rd, too, is serious if much shorter. It is called *Big Dipper* from which it may be deduced that the ground tosses and turns a great deal between tee and green (though this should be of no account as we are meant to take the aerial route). Again there is a bunker through the back of the green which, like the other bunkers on the course, is filled with a particularly handsome variety of white fluffy sand.

Thereafter it is gentler golf until the pretty 7th, a beguiling drop shot from behind the clubhouse. On first sight the prospect from the 8th tee is little less than alarming with a big tree on the left immediately in front of the tee, more trees almost straight in front and a stream zigzagging its way the length of the fairway. With first timer's luck I solved the problem with a 3-iron hit under the first tree, over the next lot and onto a patch of flat fairway from which the short pitch over the stream to the green was easy enough, but I am glad I was not required to repeat the feat!

*(MR)*

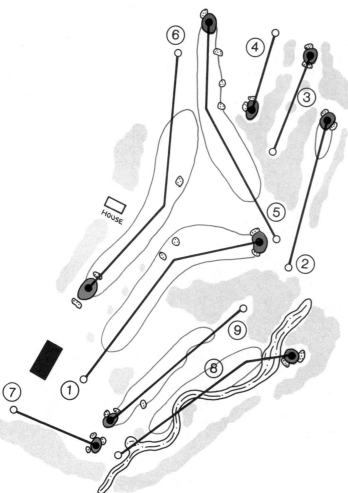

| Card of the course: | | |
|---|---|---|
| 1. | 318 yards | par 4 |
| 2. | 210 | 3 |
| 3. | 142 | 3 |
| 4. | 112 | 3 |
| 5. | 348 | 4 |
| 6. | 327 | 4 |
| 7. | 122 | 3 |
| 8. | 272 | 4 |
| 9. | 237 | 4 |
| Out: | 2088 yards | par 32 |
| Total: | 4176 yards | par 64   s.s.s. 65 |

# Plassey

*4590 yards; par 64*

$W$hen, three years ago, I wrote *Golf Courses of Cheshire (Sigma Leisure)* I visited a number of newly established courses. With one exception each of the high-budget, "instant" projects has been forced to change hands, often at the insistence of the receiver. There were other schemes, less ambitious or more cautious depending on your point of view, in which land owners turned their unprofitable farmland into golf courses gradually. Most of these seem to be flourishing, expanding only as the money comes in at a level to sustain growth, and several more have joined them since publication. Plassey is a recently formed (1992) course just inside the

Welsh border near Bangor-on-Dee which promises to develop in a similar fashion, and our hopes must go with it for already it provides a good deal of amusement at a very reasonable cost (reduced, it should be added, for guests of the nearby caravan park) and is well-suited to the difficult task of providing entertainment for a visiting party of widely mixed abilities.

The course runs over undulating meadowland to the rear of the Plassey estate, now replete with craft workshops in and around the old brewery. Until last winter there were up to 13 holes, but recent rationalisation has reduced the number to 9 partly to improve routing and safety and also to ensure one or two fuller-length par-4s. The layout is still being developed, greens being enlarged and tees better sited, so the card and map quoted here may change a little over the coming years. This account is of the March 1996 version.

As the round progresses things tighten up somewhat, so advantage should be taken of the gentle par-4s which open proceedings before it is necessary to strike out strongly over a deep, river-filled valley to find the 3rd green. The card suggests that it is only 162 yards from tee to flag, but I suspect that either any future remeasuring will adjust that figure upwards or my 5-iron needs replacing!

Another invigorating carry is in prospect from the 4th tee, once a left-handed *cape* hole up into the

**Plassey 7th**

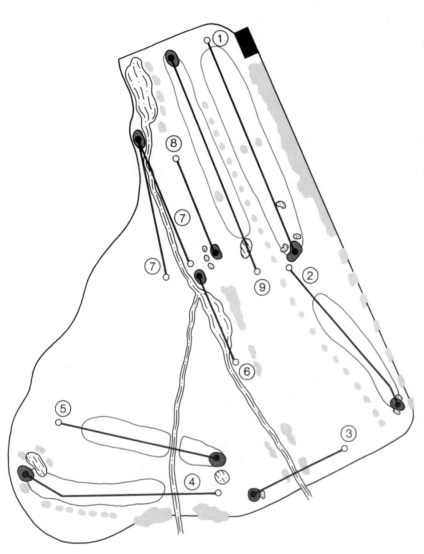

corner but now longer and working to the right towards a green squeezed between a pond and a big tree, not at all an easy target to find from the wrong angle. The 5th is more or less the same thing in reverse before a couple of very attractive and seductive sirens follow, both of them short holes along the river valley to narrow greens tilting towards the water. There are no safe options here. Neither does it pay to miss the 8th green, a tiny ledge green on the side of a hill. Finally the 9th works its way along a sloping hillside fairway to a green overlooking a small lake. This green is scheduled for reconstruction, making it more receptive to the long approach shots that most of us will need having deliberately kept the driver in the bag for fear of failing to hold the narrow fairway.

*(MR)*

### Card of the course:

| | | |
|---|---|---|
| 1. | 360 yards | par 4 |
| 2. | 280 | 4 |
| 3. | 162 | 3 |
| 4. | 315 | 4 |
| 5. | 287 | 4 |
| 6. | 146 | 3 |
| 7. | 215 | 3 |
| 8. | 165 | 3 |
| 9. | 365 | 4 |
| Out: | 2295 yards | par 32 |
| Total: | 4590 yards | par 64 |

# *Porthmadog*

*6363 yards; par 71; s.s.s. 71*

O how the years roll on! I find it hard to believe that thirty years have gone by since my first game at Porthmadog. During that time I have played a great many rounds on this ever improving course. As a traditionalist I often think that changes, either by choice or of necessity, are not always for the best. At Porthmadog, however, the changes have generally enhanced the course's qualities.

The course is about five minutes' drive from the bustling little town of Porthmadog at Morfa Bychan. It was founded in 1905 and known then as the Porthmadog and Borth-y-Gest Golf Club.

Having consulted Mr. Lever, the Harlech professional, who was of the opinion that for an expenditure of £80 a good sporting links of nine holes could be secured on the land that contained large areas of gorse, sand dunes and wet hollows, work commenced in mid-March 1906 and, despite only having half-crown picks and shovels and a horse and cart, remarkably the course was ready for play by the end of May that same year! The course rules were very strict and golfers were required to be on their best behaviour and in particular were not to take away any hares, rabbits or wildfowl and

**Porthmadog 14th**

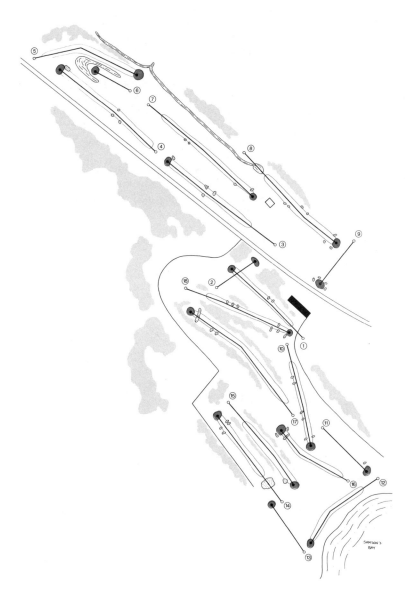

they were required to pay full compensation for any sheep, cattle or other animal killed or injured by them. They were most definitely not to play golf on Sundays nor to diminish the level of water in Llyn Samson.

Try as I did, through numerous channels, I never did discover when the course was extended to a full eighteen holes but by 1912 it was described as a fully equipped club. Certainly that year was memorable for the club's professional, Evan Jones, as his work load was lightened by the appointment of a greenkeeper. No longer did Evan have to work from dawn to dusk cutting the greens and tees with a hand mower, filling the sand-boxes and repairing the boundary fences in addition to the more customary duties of a professional. I am sure that my long-standing friend, Peter Bright, the club's current professional, is also relieved that these duties are no longer in the job description!

The opening hole would appear to be a relatively simple par-4 according to the card. No such luck! To the out-of-bounds have recently been added fairway bunkers and there is a ditch just short of the green to grab the badly struck second shot. Early drama could, so easily, unfold. The ditch plays its part again along with plentiful trouble left and right of the short 2nd hole.

It is across the road, then, to begin a seven hole stretch which I should not describe as true links. A par-5 is the first hole with which to contend here. Drive off with caution, as the line from the tee favours the right-hand rough. The following three holes, two par-4s and a par-3, have only been in existence for a few years, yet what a different dimension they have brought to the course! The 4th, thwart with danger to its left, is a tough two-shotter with its slightly undulating fairway as the green is approached and a putting surface to match. This is followed by a severe dog-leg right, its main feature being a pond to the right of the fairway. Anything short of a perfect carry and the ball comes to rest in an aquatic grave.

Having played the second short hole, two par-5s follow, the first of which has a couple of newly appointed pot-bunkers somewhat unfairly positioned, thus punishing the well-played tee shot. The next par-5 is in stark contrast. Well-positioned traps to the right and an out-of-bounds on the left call for a testing tee shot. Course management is then the order of the day for the long second shot to a high-rise green, and what a green it is, sloping with its subtle borrows! Approaching the half-way mark, from an elevated tee, the short 9th with its big green is guarded by traps and water.

It is a couple of minutes' walk to the 10th tee but I assure you it is well worthwhile as we approach a glorious links layout over the back nine. Pin-point accuracy from the tee avoids out-of-bounds left-side and gorse bushes to the right, and as on the drive so with the second shot to the green with its narrow entrance and astutely placed traps. Then comes the 11th, which is far from being my favourite hole on the course. Miss the green on the right and you could be left with an awkward sandy lie for the pitch to the small green while only a little too far left and it is three off the tee. All this at 220-yards plus!

Samson Bay, threatened with coastal erosion over the years, makes for a fine feature on the short but tricky par-4 12th. As a first time player here full respect must be given to the hole. May I recommend a long-iron from the tee down to the low-lying fairway rather than some hit-and-hope drive which may well prove catastrophic? Samson's Bay is a popular little cove for the holiday-maker, whom I am sure must wonder at the huge boulder hanging precariously on the cliff face. Folk lore would have us believe that Samson hurled that very boulder from the cliff top.

It is a short hike from this green to the course's highest point with the tee of the 13th situated up behind the previous green. The finest views are from here looking across Tremadog Bay towards the whole expanse of the Snowdonia mountain range and the town of Harlech with its cliff-top castle on the far side of the estuary. The hole itself, with its punchbowl green, requires another long and accurate carry, any amount of trouble awaiting the mis-hit.

With five holes to play, the *Himalayas*, as the next hole is known, fully justifies its Stroke Index 1 rating. The tee shot is awesome with a huge sandy waste to carry to a blind fairway. So often as I have walked down this fairway my mind has gone back a quarter of a century to when this hole was played as a short par-4 dog-legging left to a punch-bowl green tucked away in the sand hills. Now there is a most demanding second shot in order to avoid strategically placed bunkers and an out-of-bounds.

Most golfers come away with a favourite hole on this course and the 15th, *Pen-y-Boncan*, gets my vote with its swelling fairway and much gorse to cope with from the drive and still further trouble ahead. It is a demanding second shot to find the plateau (and slight Mackenzie) green nestling up in the hillside. Again radical changes took place at this hole several years ago. Then, teeing up close to Samson Bay, the 16th is perhaps the easiest par-4 on the course. Until recently the penultimate hole, *Ty Isac*, was a beast of a par-4 with its gorse-lined fairway, calling for two mighty strikes to the heart of the green. Perhaps it was too difficult for the majority in this form. Lately it has been altered and is now a par-5 with a ditch running just short of the green.

Standing on the 18th tee the memories came flooding back once again as the line for the drive used to be the fluorescent signs in the window of the professional's old shop in the far distance. Times have changed and three new bunkers are in place to swallow up the drive left of the fairway. It is a deceptive second shot and so easy to underclub the approach to this well-guarded and tricky final green. It was good to revisit Porthmadog and it provides an ideal opportunity for me to thank, in print, the members of this club for their warm hospitality on numerous occasions over the years.

*(PL)*

### Card of the course:

| No. | Yards | Par | No. | Yards | Par |
|---|---|---|---|---|---|
| 1. | 360 yards | par 4 | 10. | 378 yards | par 4 |
| 2. | 172 | 3 | 11. | 221 | 3 |
| 3. | 503 | 5 | 12. | 360 | 4 |
| 4. | 459 | 4 | 13. | 203 | 3 |
| 5. | 390 | 4 | 14. | 389 | 4 |
| 6. | 143 | 3 | 15. | 382 | 4 |
| 7. | 511 | 5 | 16. | 331 | 4 |
| 8. | 482 | 5 | 17. | 498 | 5 |
| 9. | 180 | 3 | 18. | 401 | 4 |
| Out: | 3200 yards | par 36 | | | |
| In: | 3163 yards | par 35 | | | |
| Total: | 6363 yards | par 71 | s.s.s. 71 | | |

# *Prestatyn*

*6564 yards; par 72; s.s.s. 72*

Almost every new golf course appearing on the scene today is advertised as a "Championship Layout". I am sure it entices potential new members to acquire their debentures or to purchase their time-share chalets but you know and I know that there are very few *true* championships to go round and most still are held on long-established courses of proven pedigree. Prestatyn is no pretender, having hosted such august events as the Welsh Amateur Championship, Welsh Amateur Stroke Play and Welsh Ladies

**Prestatyn 11th**

Amateur. It has tested the best golfers at the east end of the promenade since the turn of the century. It is a links course though, strangely enough, more recognisably so on the inland part from the 11th onwards. Up to that point the golf is undeniably flat, but then so is the golf at Royal Liverpool and no one is going to gainsay the greatness of that historic links. The well-known North Wales golfer Sid Collins was responsible for the design of the course as we know it today and in recent years improvements and modifications were carried out by Donald Steel, while extension and refurbishment of the clubhouse have ensured that members and visitors alike are as comfortable off the course as they are tested on it.

The immediate effect of the opening ten holes is similar to neighbouring Rhyl just along the coast or Leasowe only a few miles distant – if you have a boat – over on the Wirral coast between Hoylake and Wallasey. On each of these the sea is barely visible from the course despite its proximity. The serious golfer, I dare say, is not to be distracted by mere marine views and he will appreciate all too readily the potentially devastating effects of the wind. A great deal will depend on the tees from which the golfer is playing for there is a difference of nearly 600 yards to the length of the course as played from the visitors' yellow tees and the blue championship markers when the course measures 6,808 yards with a Standard Scratch of 73.

The budding champion must decide whether to attempt the drive to the 1st green or not. It is easy enough as a par-4 if you aim right and then pitch in over the bunker, but if you seek glory you must drive over the rough which skirts a ditch on the direct line and hope to squeeze between the two bunkers separating you from the flag. All is plainly visible from the tee. You may have greater difficulty identifying the best line over the next few holes. This may be infuriating, but it is an essential part of true seaside golf where, traditionally, there are no trees or the like to aid the judgement of distance. In the heat haze of summer, a low winter sun, or with tears brought to the eyes by a Force 8 neither the 2nd nor the 3rd is easy to judge, especially the 3rd with its challenge of a ditch and out-of-bounds fence on the second shot.

Even the strongest hitters will find themselves at full stretch on the 4th, the second shot required to cross a low ridge to find the green. You may be able to see the top of the flag as you play this shot but you will certainly not be able to see the bottom. Of the greenside bunkers you would be wise to avoid the left-hand one if you have any choice in the matter. If you only just creep in you

may be left with no backswing and be forced to escape sideways or even backwards.

Now you are journeying all along the dunes forming the sea wall and the golf is routine enough until you play the new version of the 7th. A green has been constructed in the dunes about 50 yards nearer the sea than the existing green. Once all one had to do was keep out of the bunkers on the right and miss the ditch further on. Now you will want just to pass close by those fairway bunkers to stand any chance of getting your second shot airborne long enough to clear the Apache territory between you and the green. The beauty of the hole is that the safer you play with your second shot the trickier the pitch you are left with. The 8th takes play out to the end of this part of the course, simply enough from the yellow tee but rather more sternly from the blue one when the long second shot must be played over all sorts of bumpy ground to find the green in a sheltered corner.

Striking back parallel, the outward half ends with a short par-4 which would be quite unremarkable were it not for the little stream which flows round three sides of the green. There is no alternative to a pitch which lands on exactly the right part of the green and stays there. There is a ridge separating the front and back portions of the green – what you might call a *reverse* Mackenzie – and it pays to do a little research before playing the shot. Were you playing from the blue tees you would have covered almost 3,600 yards so far.

The greater challenge for most of us is still to come as we meet up with the *gutter* running alongside the 10th. I should be inclined to think of it less as a gutter and more as a full-scale canal and it is a real threat to driving from the 10th tee, and that may be the better side to be to avoid the fairway bunkers and also to give a view of the green past the mound which projects into the fairway from the right. For good measure the practice ground is just to the right of the fairway and out-of-bounds. Hit over the *gutter* to find the 11th green, and clear the several bunkers and ridge on the direct line. This is a real seaside special and to prove the point there is a sinister little bunker hidden from view just off the putting surface to the right.

From here on the course runs alongside the railway and this is grand links territory which could so easily have been lifted from Rye or Hunstanton. The 12th makes a long trek out between hillocks littered with innumerable bunkers on the right and the dreaded *gutter* on the left. At the far end the 13th climbs over very

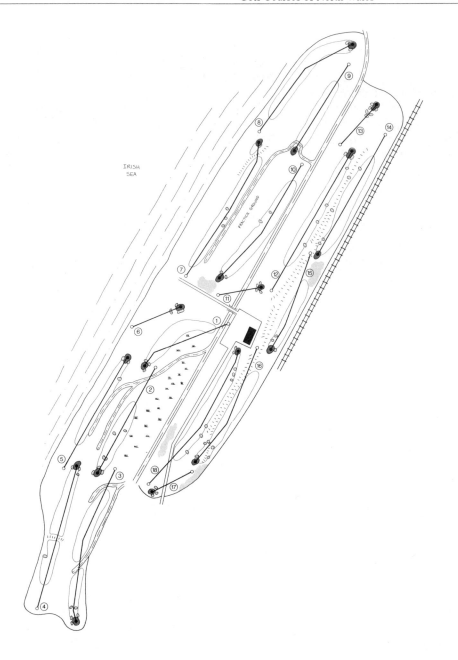

bumpy ground and half a dozen bunkers to a green up on top of a pinnacle. It may be hard to hit this green from the tee but it may be even harder to hit it from one or other of the dreadful lies in the depressions below it.

Right up by the railway on the 14th tee we have to ensure that the drive lands neither on the tracks nor in one of the many bunkers on the right. If anything, the second shot is more disturbing with a ridge to be crossed some way short of the green and the ground beyond tending to throw the ball off into the left rough. Again approach shots seem to veer left on the shorter 15th but that is the end of the railway. Instead a car park performs a similar golfing function as the most dangerous threat on the 16th, a drive and mid-iron from the yellow plates but almost a par-$4\frac{1}{2}$ from the championship tee with the green raised up on a plateau well beyond the bunkers and ridge which contrive to make it seem closer than it really is.

You passed the 17th green as you drove in, little more than a drop shot over bunkers with the threat of an out-of-bounds fence just through the back. What an interesting collection of short holes Prestatyn has! You also crossed the 18th and the road marks the out-of-bounds for much of the fairway's length. There are bunkers on the right to balance this and the fairway undulates markedly until at the end it is separated by almost a dry moat from the green which has a couple of attendant bunkers below it on the left.

A plainer championship course than Harlech or Conwy, for sure, but the real thing never the less, Prestatyn is a place to try in a winter easterly when holes such as the 4th and 7th become a real handful and it will take three very substantial shots to reach the 12th in regulation. Play the course in the prevailing wind from the west and the 10th, 14th and 16th more than justify their stroke ratings though you may then fancy your chances of sneaking one back on the 18th.

*(MR)*

### Card of the course:

| | | | | | |
|---|---|---|---|---|---|
| 1. | 307 yards | par 4 | 10. | 450 yards | par 4 |
| 2. | 382 | 4 | 11. | 139 | 3 |
| 3. | 516 | 5 | 12. | 507 | 5 |
| 4. | 468 | 4 | 13. | 175 | 3 |
| 5. | 404 | 4 | 14. | 434 | 4 |
| 6. | 176 | 3 | 15. | 335 | 4 |
| 7. | 490 | 5 | 16. | 414 | 4 |
| 8. | 412 | 4 | 17. | 150 | 3 |
| 9. | 311 | 4 | 18. | 494 | 5 |

| | | | |
|---|---|---|---|
| Out: | 3466 yards | par 37 | |
| In: | 3098 yards | par 35 | |
| Total: | 6564 yards | par 72 | s.s.s. 72 |

# Pwllheli

*6091 yards; par 69; s.s.s. 69*

One can feel quite envious of the members of Pwllheli who have such a glorious and challenging course on the south-east coast of the Lleyn Peninsula. I am sure a century ago it was this perfect setting which induced the Cardiff-based Solomon Andrew family to approach Tom Morris to lay out a 9-hole private course. The club was formed in 1900 and the nine holes were soon found to be inadequate. More land was obtained and the first 18-hole course designed and laid out in 1908/9 by James Braid. The course was opened by the Rt. Hon. David Lloyd George on the 1st June 1909 who, in return, was given Honorary Membership and the club's president announced that he also had the freedom of the club's facilities but not the whisky! This brought raucous laughter from the gallery.

In the 1920s the club leased a parkland area and incorporated

**Pwllheli 11th**

the new holes into the best of Braid's links. The new course was opened by Arthur Havers during his year as Open Champion. The course is hardly changed except for the 3rd, 4th and 5th holes which were designed by local enthusiasts in 1973. Pwllheli is, then, one of those rare courses blessed with a rich collection of both seaside and inland golf, its first seven holes being parkland with lush fairways stimulated by their clay base. The links section begins to unfold from the 8th, running parallel with one of the many sandy beaches for which this area is famous, making Pwllheli such a popular holiday resort. Thus the layout of the course is predominantly governed by its boundaries of water: the shores of Cardigan Bay on the one side and the meandering Penrhos River on the other. Although my most recent visit took place in February it was a gloriously calm and sunny day and I felt privileged to be able to savour the delights and splendour of the course and its surroundings under such conditions. This is one of the great things about seaside golf in this part of the world – it can be every bit as glorious in mid-winter as in mid-summer.

The first of the parkland holes is a good opener to the round. It is of medium length and as straight as a Roman road. A number of factors prove difficult on the testing 2nd hole. A drive through the ever-thickening trees needs to favour the left side of the rippling and narrowing fairway. Out-of-bounds awaits an over-zealous approach to the green. It is target golf at its best on the short 3rd with its raised island green surrounded by a deep depression. If that is not enough to create difficulties, a large bunker sits at the front left side of the green.

Holes 4, 5 and 6 run parallel to each other, the first of which plays the most difficult with trees and bushes lining the right of the fairway for well over half the length of the hole. Trees again are very prevalent to the sides and back of the green. The 5th, although not long for a par-4, is no pushover with its tree-lined fairway and man-made pond fronting the green. Faced with an intrepid approach shot to the green, an over-eager pitch could come to rest in a hidden bunker at the back of the green. The next is a fairly straightforward hole except for a two-tier green. The 7th, heading back to the clubhouse, is a bold par-4 with trees down its right side and a water hazard stretching almost the full length of the hole on the left. Pay close attention to the ditch which crosses the fairway 100 yards short of the green.

Then it is out with the new and in with the old as we approach the 8th, the opening to the links part of the course. It is tight, with gorse here, there and everywhere plus extremely well-positioned bunkers ready to snaffle up anything but the best of second shots to the undulating green. To add to the frustration there is a path, which also haunts the 9th and 10th holes, from which no relief is given other than under the "one stroke penalty" rule. Approaching the half-way mark the wide open 9th fairway will fill you with confidence for the drive, but that feeling could soon ebb away should you fail to negotiate the twin grass walls positioned across the fairway 30 yards from the green. Under-clubbing could prove costly.

A classic short hole makes the 10th one to remember, not only because of the delightful black and white cottage situated behind the green but also for the well-guarded and cunningly laid out green. Having climbed up to the elevated 11th tee there are breath-taking views of Abersoch to the south-west with the Pembrokeshire coast due south in the very far distance and the Snowdonia range rising inland. Having relished the glorious surroundings it would be easy to allow concentration to lapse when playing this short par-4, but what folly that would be! There is a mass of trouble to the left in the form of gorse and marram grass and also a number of splendidly appointed bunkers particularly around the green.

Having played the short 12th, the 13th could be unlucky for some with its tee cunningly repositioned a few years ago, making the hole into a subtle dog-leg. The drive is daunting, to say the least, with trees, gorse and a water hazard flanking the left side of the fairway. Anything but an accurately struck second shot will make par an unlikely proposition. The severe right-hand dog-leg 14th can be a ball of confusion. There is ample room leftside for a well-placed tee shot but there is also a great temptation to drive the

ball round the dog-leg and out-of-bounds can easily take its toll. The green is wide but short and a man-made pond awaits anything short left and the River Penrhos any shot too long. Should you come away from the 14th free from any penalty shots you are all set up to face up to a hole where trouble abounds on all sides. There is a river and gorse all the way round the dog-leg left, a couple of cross-ditches ready to catch the mis-hit drive and gorse to the right leaving a demanding shot to a well-bunkered green.

The 16th, my favourite hole on the course, is another dog-leg left swathed in gorse on both sides of the rolling fairway. Taking the marker post as the ideal line from the tee you are then left with a tricky pitch to an undulating and well-protected green.

We move away from the links on the 17th with its lush fairway. A line of tall trees to the right makes the favourable line for the drive left of centre. A ridge across the neck of the fairway can make the second shot to a shallow green most deceiving. The final hole, a modest-looking par-4, has a broad fairway and a number of bunkers and hummocks surrounding a large green. It makes for a pleasant end to this not overly long course without a single par-5, yet Pwllheli provides a splendid game for all golfing levels.

*(PL)*

| Card of the course: | | | | | |
|---|---|---|---|---|---|
| 1. | 382 yards | par 4 | 10. | 197 yards | par 3 |
| 2. | 423 | 4 | 11. | 291 | 4 |
| 3. | 146 | 3 | 12. | 146 | 3 |
| 4. | 377 | 4 | 13. | 413 | 4 |
| 5. | 317 | 4 | 14. | 342 | 4 |
| 6. | 339 | 4 | 15. | 455 | 4 |
| 7. | 441 | 4 | 16. | 347 | 4 |
| 8. | 350 | 4 | 17. | 374 | 4 |
| 9. | 400 | 4 | 18. | 351 | 4 |
| Out: | 3175 yards | par 35 | | | |
| In: | 2916 yards | par 34 | | | |
| Total: | 6091 yards | par 69 | | s.s.s. 69 | |

# Rhos-on-Sea

*6064 yards; par 69; s.s.s. 69*

The seaside town of Rhos-on-Sea lies along the sandy coast line between bustling Colwyn Bay, backed by wooded green hills leading into some of Wales's most beautiful scenery, and Llandudno, queen of resorts. Rhos is order, harmony and a throwback to a more genteel age. The golf course lies a little way to the west separated from the sea only by the coast road and the sea defences. Founded in 1899 this compact, mostly flat course is not overtaxing which makes it an ideal holiday course for those who seek relaxation rather than a tough examination. It *has* had its exciting times, however, not least back on August 10th 1910 when an aeroplane an hour and a quarter out from Blackpool suddenly landed on the course in the early morning. Whether this landing was intentional is not known, but its next landing, on the town of Cemlyn, was sadly disastrous.

The known history of the course is rather vague, though the distinguished Tom Simpson's company was called in for an update in 1934. The site will have contrasted greatly with that of Ballybunion on which he was also working around this time, the latter playing through as monumental a set of dunes as you will find anywhere. It is interesting to note that when they measured the course at Rhos they found it 200 yards longer than the card indicated. I bet a few members could have told them that without the need for measurement!

Internal out-of-bounds comes into play on several holes (hardly everybody's cup of tea!) and there are several stretches of water running through the middle of the course. This is very low ground, close to, or even below, sea level, and those stretches of water are part of the necessary drainage system keeping the fairways dry, but the water

*Rhos-on-Sea 3rd*

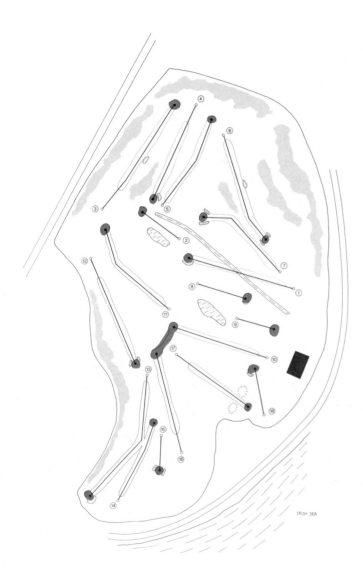

IRISH SEA

is not far below the surface and bunkers are not easy to maintain under such circumstances, so there are very few to be encountered during the round. Instead a number of the greens are raised up above dry moats making them harder to hit and hold than appearances suggest.

Highlighting one or two holes, the 3rd is the first to come to mind, a slightly uphill par-5 which demands a straight drive as out-of-bounds and a lateral water hazard flank play but the main feature of the hole is its tricky punchbowl green. Holes 8 and 9, a couple of par-3s on the bounce, are played with significant water problems, the water being home to several species of wildlife.

The 13th is a par-5, utterly simple in design and strategy, yet worthy of a place on any course in North Wales. A dog-leg right with all sorts of trouble down the right side, it has a well-protected green. Playing the 16th you might be reminded of the Old Course at St. Andrews with its double green shared with the 10th. The 17th is not long but the approach shot must be precise, the green blind on the far side of a mound, this time a nod in the direction of the New Course. The round ends with a gentle par-3, perhaps not a remarkable hole in itself, but one which leaves no room for error if the match is to be decided by the outcome of this one hole.

(PL)

### Card of the course:

| | | | | | |
|---|---|---|---|---|---|
| 1. | 413 yards | par 4 | 10. | 396 yards | par 4 |
| 2. | 168 | 3 | 11. | 370 | 4 |
| 3. | 492 | 5 | 12. | 413 | 4 |
| 4. | 395 | 4 | 13. | 543 | 5 |
| 5. | 400 | 4 | 14. | 346 | 4 |
| 6. | 408 | 4 | 15. | 138 | 3 |
| 7. | 387 | 4 | 16. | 367 | 4 |
| 8. | 175 | 3 | 17. | 336 | 4 |
| 9. | 141 | 3 | 18. | 176 | 3 |
| Out: | 2979 yards | par 34 | | | |
| In: | 3085 yards | par 35 | | | |
| Total: | 6064 yards | par 69 | s.s.s. 69 | | |

# *Rhuddlan*

*6482 yards; par 71; s.s.s. 71*

To the student of historical architecture Rhuddlan Castle might be considered a set work, the first of Edward I's concentric fortresses. Started in 1277 it was the king's principal stronghold for his conquest of North Wales and a forerunner of those other great bastions at Conwy, Harlech and Beaumaris. It is said to have been Queen Eleanor's favourite castle and it is claimed that it was at Rhuddlan that the first English Prince of Wales was created. The River Clwyd was diverted and canalised to gives ships access to the castle from the sea, thus also giving the castle control of the main coastal route into North Wales. While non-golfers are enjoying the finer points of the castle (or the even older delights of nearby Tuthill) less committed historians might profit from 18-

*Rhuddlan 17th*

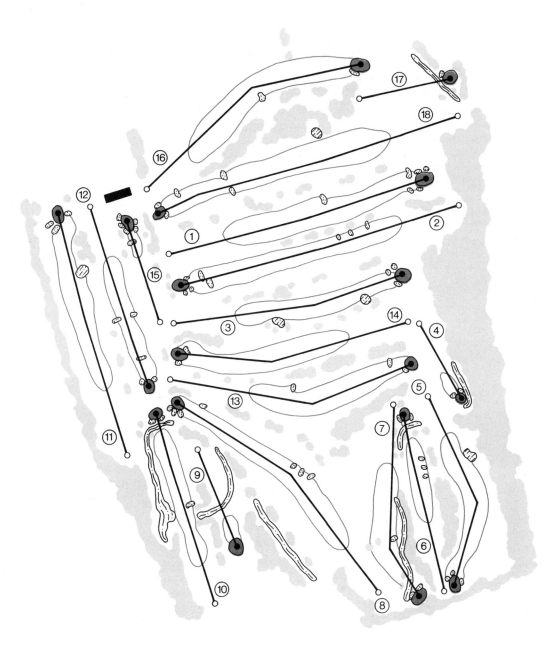

holes at nearby Rhuddlan Golf Club. Appropriately the castle features on the club's crest.

My father used greatly to enjoy his visits to Rhuddlan with the Conwy Seniors back in the late '70s and early '80s, and it was then a compact layout occupying little over 80 acres with the occasional problems of crossing holes. Rhuddlan had in the past called on the Hawtree family firm for course alterations so when an extra 35 acres became available about a decade ago it was to Hawtrees that they again turned for a rebuild. (One or two of the old greens remain and can be returned to play in adversity, a welcome aid for the greenkeeping staff, I am sure.) Hawtrees also returned recently to make further amendments to the bunkering and one or two of the older greens. As the character of the holes here is determined by the nature of the ground on which they are laid out there is some excuse for abandoning the normal consecutive description of the round and collecting them together by type instead.

Seven of the holes run in parallel over a central

tract, serious holes each of them, the long par-4s benefiting from the slight fall of ground towards a wood beyond which rises Dyserth Mountain, an imposing backdrop. These are the sort of par-4s that separate the men from the boys, low handicappers reaching for a mid-iron for their second shots, those of my limited ability failing to reach even with a fairway wood. Two of the holes returning are par-5s of sufficient length to call for robust hitting from all golfers as they climb gently towards greens raised up on the horizon. On each of these holes the success of the drive is greatly determined by the clumps of trees around which the fairways bend mildly to left or right. There are not too many trees on this part of the course but the few there are are utilised to good effect. One of these holes, the present 14th, was created out of two former holes, the second of which was apparently a treacherous par-3 across the corner of a cricket field. The new hole is not only fairer but also blessed with an intriguing green, stepped and sloping from right to left.

It is followed by an innocuous looking short hole, the 15th, yet the Secretary-Manager tells me his office just beyond the green is bombarded surprisingly frequently. Once you have fallen foul of the astutely positioned bunkers towards the front of this green you begin to appreciate why. Of the other par-3s the 4th is straightforward in a wooded corner and the 9th attractive with its tee shot played over a ditch and past a big tree on the right. The 17th is a very recently created hole and its green is just the other side of a stream demanding perfect club selection. It is a charming hole, too, down beside the fields, set off against the mountain background.

The holes around the middle of the round are all quite new (or, at least, newly altered) and they begin with the 5th, a neat dog-leg round trees with a green in front of a cottage. The 6th, coming back, is mainly a matter of not getting shut out by the big trees either side of a narrow opening through which the pitch shot must be played over a stream.

To describe the 7th as "full of character" is close to an understatement. The drive is played out to the right where a couple of big trees complement a bunker on the opposite side of the fairway. Even if the drive has been unimpeded the approach shot has to carry a stream and avoid its attendant bushes. The 8th (an entirely new hole) may be only just a par-5 on the card but, as I played it, into the wind it felt distinctly long, the green raised up just sufficiently to deflect wayward approaches into bunkers left or bushes right.

After the short 9th comes another par-4 full of character. From the 10th tee the drive is threatened by a hedge and ditch on the right and a bunker a little beyond, while another ditch runs down the left. There is a third ditch just in front of the green and the putting surface is raised and angled in such a way as to require good judgement even from close at hand.

There remains another short par-4, the 12th, and it is not too tough, but it comes as a relief after the rigours of the 11th which is, not surprisingly, Stroke 1. A big drive is necessary to make the brow of a hill on which there is a marker post. Arrow-like straightness is then called for if the long second shot is to avoid first a pond, then trees on the right and finally big greenside bunkers on the left. To lay up short of all this trouble still leaves at least a mid-iron in to the green. When the most recent alterations to the course were made (principally to make the course more resistant to low scoring by the Category 1 players) this hole, hardly surprisingly, needed no further strengthening.

*(MR)*

### Card of the course:

| No. | Yards | Par | No. | Yards | Par |
|---|---|---|---|---|---|
| 1. | 465 yards | par 4 | 10. | 341 yards | par 4 |
| 2. | 503 | 5 | 11. | 431 | 4 |
| 3. | 402 | 4 | 12. | 324 | 4 |
| 4. | 149 | 3 | 13. | 436 | 4 |
| 5. | 352 | 4 | 14. | 417 | 4 |
| 6. | 310 | 4 | 15. | 184 | 3 |
| 7. | 340 | 4 | 16. | 451 | 4 |
| 8. | 476 | 5 | 17. | 166 | 3 |
| 9. | 190 | 3 | 18. | 545 | 5 |
| Out: | 3187 yards | par 36 | | | |
| In: | 3295 yards | par 35 | | | |
| Total: | 6482 yards | par 71 | | s.s.s. 71 | |

# *Rhyl*

*6165 yards; par 70; s.s.s. 70*

*The course is one of nine holes, only one of which can be reached from the tee. It has been greatly improved. . . . Visitors (introduced) are allowed to play over the green free for two days, thereafter at a charge of five shillings per week. There is an excellent club house, where luncheon can be obtained.*

Before you rush out to obtain your two days' free golf you should note that the above is an extract from a golfing journal of 1893.

The Rhyl Golf Club had been in existence for three years then, a founder member of the Welsh Golfing Union, and, therefore, one of the oldest clubs in Wales. Shortly after the turn of the century the course had expanded to a full 18 holes and the course was rated highly. But in 1921 publication of plans to build a road from Rhyl to Gronant began a long period of uncertainty for the club. First they lost holes at the west end and by 1930 the course had been separated from its clubhouse by half a mile. Further land was obtained nearer to Prestatyn, James Braid advising on the design

**Rhyl 2nd**

and construction of the replacement course. Then came the Second World War and with it further loss of land. First the sea eroded parts of the coastline and in the process destroyed Salem Bungalow[*] through the grounds of which golfers passed to get from one part of the course to the next. The sea had moved inland some 550 yards between 1911 and the end of the war so a new sea defence system with promenade was built ensuring survival of the golf course but eating into it a little more. As if that were not enough, blown sand obliterated several holes at the Prestatyn end. When thought was given to restoring the golf course in peacetime there was no longer sufficient ground to accommodate a full 18 holes.

Nor are these the only tribulations this proud club has had to overcome. In the 1960s there was the threat of a huge amusement park to be built on the land, and in the club's centenary year, of all years, a combination of exceptional winds and high tides caused the course to be flooded with sea water and shortly after that a fire destroyed part of the clubhouse. It is against this background that we should be very thankful that we are able to play at all on this historic turf.

It would be as well to let the match in front putt out before teeing off at the 1st for your opening drive might well threaten the green, particularly in summer when this crispest of links turf gives almost limitless roll to the well-struck shot. Even from close at hand pitching is a matter of some skill, the green small and tightly guarded by bunkers. I remember playing here some years ago and noticing how speedy and true the putting surfaces were – a traditional seaside defence. The 2nd is similar but this time there is an internal out-of-bounds on the right to balance the menace of the sea wall on the left. The 3rd is a prime links par-3, the exact distance to the green difficult to judge with ridges and bumps all round to confuse the eye and give all manner of uncertain lies if you miss the putting surface. There is a completely separate tee when you play this hole as the 12th and approaching the green from a very different angle gives cause for thought. With the wind behind, as it often is, and the green like glass in high summer, preventing the ball shooting through the green is an art.

To play links golf well you have to cope with three factors: the wind (rarely absent and usually far stronger than you would expect to encounter inland), tight lies on close cut fairways and rolling

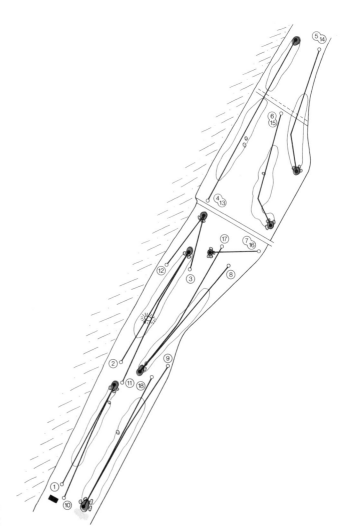

---

[*] I was told by one of my playing partners that the owner of this bungalow had designed a turntable for electric trams. How educational a round of golf can be!

fairways (meaning that the ball is frequently above or below your feet but only occasionally on the same level). All three determine the chances of reaching the 4th green in two shots despite its running with the prevailing wind. The approach to the green is trickier than you might think, too, the humps and hollows slight enough to be almost invisible but effective at disguising the true distance to the flag. Beyond is a wilderness of dunes and brambles where once this course roamed, so it is with regret that here we turn for home, and very likely into the wind it will be.

Both the 5th and 6th are appealing holes with the former menaced by an out-of-bounds cutting on the left, the drive ideally crossing a slight ridge ahead. As you pitch to this green you suddenly become aware of just how easy it would be to drag the ball onto the road alongside or to let it drift into one or other of the protecting bunkers. Then on the 6th you take aim on a distant church tower (fleeting images of St. Andrews entering the mind) striking out right before swinging left in to the green. It is possible to cut off some or most of the dog-leg but that might be better left until the second time round when you have had a chance to size up the challenge and seen how the rough has been grown in to make that a perilous option. The bunker directly in front of the green could hardly be more mischievously placed.

There is a brief respite at the 7th, a short hole playing across the course (and wind), much depending on where the hole has been cut how you try to avoid the little bunker right in front. Beware several nasty hollows through the back of the green if your enthusiasm gets too great!

From the 8th tee the next hole plays solidly, and when you return to play it from the 17th tee it has turned into a real handful.

The extra yards and the different angle second time round make finding the ideal spot very tricky from the tee. The rough has been allowed to narrow the fairway on the left while there are out-of-bounds posts along the right. The best hope of steering the approach shot onto the putting surface past two bunkers front left is to leave the drive as close to the posts as you dare. If you do have to approach from the left you will find that in playing over those bunkers you have also brought grass bunkers on the right into play. Length is at a premium on the last hole, a solitary bunker on the right being the only threat to a long drive. The second shot has to cross a series of ridges before the fairway flattens out in front of the only expansive green of the round.

*(MR)*

| Card of the course: | | | | | |
|---|---|---|---|---|---|
| 1. | 318 yards | par 4 | 10. | 346 yards | par 4 |
| 2. | 386 | 4 | 11. | 417 | 4 |
| 3. | 157 | 3 | 12. | 173 | 3 |
| 4. | 527 | 5 | 13. | 524 | 5 |
| 5. | 358 | 4 | 14. | 356 | 4 |
| 6. | 332 | 4 | 15. | 334 | 4 |
| 7. | 141 | 3 | 16. | 129 | 3 |
| 8. | 389 | 4 | 17. | 419 | 4 |
| 9. | 457 | 4 | 18. | 402 | 4 |
| Out: | 3065 yards | par 35 | | | |
| In: | 3100 yards | par 35 | | | |
| Total: | 6165 yards | par 70 | | s.s.s. 70 | |

# Royal St. David's

*6495 yards; par 69; s.s.s. 72*

It seems amazing that the seed for this prestigious golf club was sown on one day in the 1890s when a Mr. W.H. More, from his balcony, saw a figure far below on the wastelands of Harlech engaged in a strange form of exercise. Curiosity getting the better of him, he discovered a young man hurling a boomerang. Deep conversation followed and the young man introduced himself as Harold Finch-Hatton who had recently returned from Australia. A number of days later Mr. More spotted him engaged in an even stranger pursuit and on investigation Finch-Hatton said, "Capital place for a golf links; come on let's lay one out!" and that is exactly what they did.

Having heard of the pre-eminence of St. Andrews in Scottish golf and aware that the English had a St. George's golf club at Sandwich, it seemed to the founders the name, St. David's, was logical and appropriate for this new Welsh enterprise which was launched on 1st November 1894. Officially St. David's became *Royal* in 1909 although the club used the title from 1897 when Edward, the Prince of Wales, became patron of the club, but they were told in no uncertain terms that a royal patron did not automatically give a royal status.

Royal St. David's is the jewel in the crown of golf courses throughout North Wales, its links shadowed by a canvas of sheer beauty. In the foreground stands the old ruined castle crowning the rock in its understated magnificence, surrounded by splendid countryside. In the background is the continuous outline of the Snowdonia range which can be seen from almost every point on the links. The area between the castle and the sea, the morfa, has lent itself naturally to this superb course, the large expanse of sand dunes giving shelter from the sea.

It is some feat that within five years of the idea for the development of this course it had become established as one of the principal golfing resorts of the kingdom, a position it has held to this day. If one has to single out one person for this success it has to be William Henry More who initially knew nothing about the sport and later played only rarely. An article in the *Morning Post* of 1930 written by Arthur Croome (the Radley schoolmaster, fine amateur player and architect of one of the finest inland courses in the south of England, Liphook) described More as the eighth of the seven wonders of the world. One of More's great philosophies – and I would tend to agree – is that the backbone of the game is the men and women of no great skill but enormous enthusiasm.

Many famous names have been associated with the club including David Lloyd George who was accused of not paying his green fee, something of an embarrassment as he was Chancellor of the Exchequer at the time! Possibly the feather in the cap is Edward VIII who, as Prince of Wales, accepted the captaincy in 1934. In addition, Harold Hilton, twice winner of the Open, four times Amateur Champion and the last Englishman to take the U.S. Amateur, promoted Royal St. David's in the many articles he wrote for golfing journals. The presence of the golfing aristocracy influenced Harlech considerably and it became a magnet for visitors from both the business and academic worlds. Patric Dickinson saw fit to include Harlech in his select eighteen courses which made up *A Round of Golf Courses*, his 1951 classic recently reprinted. The "peculiarly happy, carefree atmosphere" he noted then remains to this day, as does the serenity and tranquillity identified by many in the earliest days, adding to the enjoyment of play on this course.

Work went on relentlessly to perfect the course and in 1896 it held its first inter-club matches, against Harborne (Birmingham) and Aberdovey, and both matches were won. In 1897 they had 92 entrants for their summer meeting with players coming from as far afield as St. Andrews, Felixstowe and Hoylake. It was felt that the St. David's Club had arrived. The individuality of the club at the turn of the century is demonstrated by an anecdote about the gardener/greenkeeper. He had taken to the bottle and was often found horizontal on the course dressed in a pink hunting coat, his badge of office. The committee brought in a local rule that any ball landing near this prostrate figure could be dropped two clubs' lengths away without penalty.

After the 1st World War the club consolidated and felt that radical changes should be made to the course. The golf course architect, C.W. Limouzin, was commissioned to draw up plans and these suggested large changes, but after much deliberation the committee decided that they would only make essential cosmetic amendments to tighten the links. These were completed in time for the inaugural Welsh Championship meeting in 1922. This proved to be a momentous occasion which has gone down in history not

so much for the competition on the course as for Captain Ernest Carter's famous assault with golf balls on the castle. Standing near the 1st tee, around 180 yards from the castle which stood about 200 feet above him, he wagered bets of 100-1 that he could hit the castle walls. He succeeded with several drives and this is a feat not achieved since!

The club turned to Harry Colt for advice in 1924 and his most noticeable change was to the 17th on which he introduced a cross-bunker and other hazards which made this one of the best penultimate holes in British golf. The effect of the changes brought about by the distinguished architect, Charles Lawrie, in 1973 were

*Royal St. David's 18th*

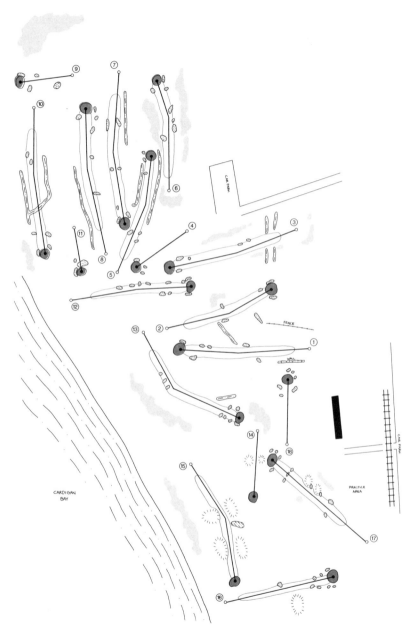

CARDIGAN
BAY

very much commented upon during the Home Internationals of 1974, particularly the green-side bunkers and toughening up of the rough. A few changes have occurred since that time, notably two new bunkers at the 3rd and raising the 14th green. Although the second nine are generally considered too short for perfection the Captain of the British P.G.A., David Huish, in 1987 stated emphatically that Harlech was the most difficult par-69 in the world. It is not surprising, therefore, that there have been numerous Welsh Championships, Ladies' British Championships, and Ladies' and Men's Home Internationals. The honours board includes the names of three Open Champions, five Amateur Champions and a Masters Champion.

The walk to the clubhouse across the railway line fills one with an air of expectation, with a feeling that time has stood still, in a similar way to the links at Aberdovey. It is wise on the opening hole to play down the left side of the fairway due to a pair of well-positioned bunkers ready to gather up a short and only slightly wayward second shot. Many greens here have umpteen subtle borrows and the 1st green sets the pattern. The 2nd hole, with a hint of a dog-leg left, guarded by a trio of green-side bunkers needs to be played according to the card's yardage: it appears shorter.

With two holes played, the next, a long, unyielding par-4 with out-of-bounds to its right and numerous strategically placed bunkers, is a force to be reckoned with. Then it is across the road to the 4th where the smallest target on the links sits 188 yards away from the tee. The challenge here is not just hitting the green but also coping with its twists and turns. On the 5th the emphasis is on a well-placed tee shot, with bunkers both left and right only too eager to collect a slightly wayward drive.

Challenging holes come aplenty on this tough yet fair links, and the 6th is no exception with gorse bushes on both sides and numerous bunkers to deal with during play on the first half of the hole and four more bunkers defending this tricky, rolling green. The course's two par-5s follow each other on holes 7 and

8. Although both are plentifully trapped through the fairways and around the greens the latter, provided you maintain a line down the left of the fairway, plays somewhat easier. Nestling alongside the perimeter of the course, and at the furthest point from the clubhouse, lies a classic par-3 with a slightly raised and uphill green. Should you be faced with a downhill putt or one across the green nothing but an adroit stroke will save you from despair.

The wind, as on any links course, can create havoc and the back nine with its strict par of 33 is the most ruthless of challenges. Just look at the length of the par-4s – only one of them under 427 yards! Although many would consider the 10th to be Harlech's finest hole it does not quite get my vote, but with heavy rough, a ditch across the fairway and bunkers to contend with it has been many a golfer's downfall I am sure.

A wide bunker across the front of the green and surrounding hummocks tend to foreshorten the par-3 11th hole. It is imperative to believe the yardage and club accordingly. Played from a pulpit tee, the 12th has a bevy of bunkers to the fairway's left side to catch drives only the slightest bit wayward. Further bunkers guard a treacherous, sloping green. The 13th, too, is as tough as they come with a trio of bunkers positioned on the right to swallow up the merest fade or push. Then comes the daunting task of threading a long second shot between four bunkers on the right and two on the left, very likely into the wind.

218 yards spells out the distance of the par-3 14th. There is not a sand trap in sight, nor need there be! There are trials in abundance with humps and hollows encircling the blind green and with only the marker post in the background as a guide to the line. Having left the short hole with a ring of the bell, the 15th drive from a high tee is all important in a bid to seek a combination of line and length. Across rough and mounds to the right side of the fairway is the position to go for. Again a bunkerless hole, it abounds with difficulties, with very little level ground *en route* to the blind green and, as with the previous hole, the green is surrounded by grassy mounds.

Climbing up to the elevated 16th tee the lovely sight of Tremadoc Bay comes into view. This hole is different from the rest of the course with its rising and falling fairway and a huge grassy mound to the right, and it is the shortest of the par-4s. Even having negotiated the drive safely an array of bunkers short of and around the green can make for a very deceptive second shot.

On the 17th the drive has to contend with one bunker on the left named *The Chinaman* - mystery surrounds its name – and three bunkers to the right. The traps strewn across the fairway make the second shot thoroughly intimidating, anything short of perfection being severely punished. As well as that all important carry to the green, directional accuracy is of equal importance as a collection of bunkers around the green could prove costly.

The final hole at Royal St. David's is a par-3, an unusual end to a round. There are one or two courses in this book which finish in this way, and very famous examples at Lindrick, Killarney, St. Pierre and Cascades in Virginia, site of several American national championships. In all these cases, and particularly at Royal St. David's, the short 18th makes for an exacting and exciting finish. Little did Messrs. More and Finch-Hatton realise what joys, pleasures and occasional frustrations they were to give to thousands of golfers over the years. Or did they?

*(PL)*

### Card of the course:

| No. | Distance | Par | No. | Distance | Par |
|-----|----------|-----|-----|----------|-----|
| 1. | 436 yards | par 4 | 10. | 458 yards | par 4 |
| 2. | 373 | 4 | 11. | 144 | 3 |
| 3. | 463 | 4 | 12. | 437 | 4 |
| 4. | 188 | 3 | 13. | 451 | 4 |
| 5. | 393 | 4 | 14. | 218 | 3 |
| 6. | 371 | 4 | 15. | 427 | 4 |
| 7. | 481 | 5 | 16. | 354 | 4 |
| 8. | 499 | 5 | 17. | 427 | 4 |
| 9. | 173 | 3 | 18. | 202 | 3 |
| Out: | 3377 yards | par 36 | | | |
| In: | 3118 yards | par 33 | | | |
| Total: | 6495 yards | par 69 | | s.s.s. 72 | |

# Ruthin-Pwllglas

*5362 yards; par 66; s.s.s. 66*

In *Golf Courses of Cheshire (Sigma Leisure)* I stated categorically, "Unquestionably Knutsford is the most beautiful 10-hole course in Cheshire (probably in the world, for that matter!)". I am glad I added the word *probably* for at that time I had not discovered Ruthin-Pwllglas. Neither is more beautiful than the other; each is incomparable. Knutsford is gentle parkland adjoining Tatton Park, Ruthin-Pwllglas rather more strenuous upland overlooking the Clwyd Valley and Hills. Both enjoy the benefits of fascinating golf in an entrancing setting.

Heading south out of Ruthin you soon come to the village of Pwllglas. Take your courage in your hands and turn right up one of the narrow roads leading to Efenechtyd. If you reach this hamlet you have missed the golf course which was a sharp right turn off the road you were probably on. Persevere! It is worth the effort to

**Ruthin-Pwllglas 1st**

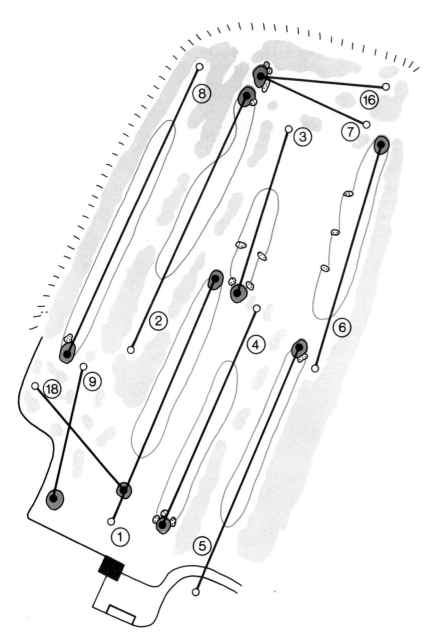

find the club. This is the only surviving course of several which once existed in the area, the Ruthin course, for instance, having failed to be resurrected after World War II, its remaining members by then affiliating themselves with the Pwllglas club which had been in existence since the 1920s, though its land had been used for golf since 1905. It runs over *Shooting Mountain*, a name which reflects the previous use of the land as a military training ground. During the Second World War the clubhouse became an officers' mess and it does not surprise the visitor to learn that for many years this was the best clubhouse for miles around, a number of other clubs which are now highly reputed then making do with little more than a tin hut. The outlook from the bar over a large part of the golf course and to the hills for miles beyond is to be savoured.

Driving off in front of the clubhouse, the 1st climbs steadily to a green on the summit of a hill from which the prospect down the Clwyd Valley towards Corwen is superb. The 2nd, too, heads in the same direction, a lovely hole played out of trees over a slight ridge and then over a shoulder of land to find the green, or *not* over the shoulder of land and into a perfectly placed bunker! Few will reach the 3rd green from the back tee except in dry weather for it is uphill all the way, but with limestone subsoil the fairways here dry quickly and good conditions prevail more frequently than you might imagine. The 4th returns to the clubhouse, first over elevated ground towards the marker post and then tumbling down over bumpy ground to a green encircled with sand.

At this point, enter my partner! The club, as friendly a club as you will find, ensured that I did not play alone and sent me out with one of their members, a lovely man who knew not only the playing of the course inside out but also each bird nesting within the boundaries and every single species of plant life. His reminiscence of the bumpy ground on the 4th was of a member who, one day, long ago, disappeared from view as he sank to his waist in one of the mine shafts which had once existed here and which everyone had forgotten about. A 6- or 7-iron will keep you well clear of this if you have driven adequately.

The 5th takes you up to the highest point on the course, 600 feet above sea level. If, by now, you have become accustomed to the splendour of the views, take care to notice that this green runs away from you (the only one of the round). Alongside the green is the tee for the *Bell Hole* on which you clang the bell *before* driving off semi-blind down the Clwyd Valley. Again the views are grand and the eye is led into the distance. If you happen to glance to your right you may notice the characteristic spotted leaves of the wild orchids which abound here. The green is down in a saucer and, as I played it, the pitch was aimed with the aid of a resplendent cock pheasant perfectly positioned on the protective rim just behind the putting surface. I suspect my partner was on first-name terms with him.

The 7th is a pretty hole through trees to a broad green set up behind a big bunker. When you return to this hole as the 16th you play it from a spectacular tee perched on the edge of the valley which falls steeply to Pwllglas far below. The longest hole, the 8th, is a beauty, driving, once again, out of a chute of trees towards a distant marker post. Though the views of the whole Clwydian

Range to the right are inspiring, there are terrible fates awaiting balls sliced out in that direction. The second shot is worth a little research as it will be blind for most of us. Separate holes of similar lengths complete each part of the round, both further uphill than they appear. In short, Ruthin-Pwllglas is a little jewel.

*(MR)*

### Card of the course:

| | | | | | |
|---|---|---|---|---|---|
| 1. | 349 yards | par 4 | 10. | 376 yards | par 4 |
| 2. | 370 | 4 | 11. | 370 | . 4 |
| 3. | 225 | 3 | 12. | 225 | 3 |
| 4. | 317 | 4 | 13. | 317 | 4 |
| 5. | 355 | 4 | 14. | 355 | 4 |
| 6. | 310 | 4 | 15. | 310 | 4 |
| 7. | 141 | 3 | 16. | 141 | 3 |
| 8. | 419 | 4 | 17. | 419 | 4 |
| 9. | 183 | 3 | 18. | 180 | 3 |
| Out: | 2669 yards | par 33 | | | |
| In: | 2693 yards | par 33 | | | |
| Total: | 5362 yards | par 66 | | s.s.s. 66. | |

# St. Deiniol

*5657 yards; par 68; s.s.s. 67*

After leaving the westbound carriageway of the A55 and travelling some two miles towards the city of Bangor the club house and part of the course is visible on the left-hand side high up on a hill. The steep incline to the golf club is quite bewildering and you could be forgiven for wondering what could possibly lie at the end of the rugged lane. I can assure you there is a fine test of golf ahead.

The course was founded in 1906 and extended to 18 holes in 1911, the work of reconstruction and extension being entrusted to James Braid, Open Champion for the fourth time at Sandwich only the year before. Then in 1915 the name of the club was changed from Bangor to St. Deiniol, the name taken from the saint who founded the original church in the 6th century. There are many

**St. Deiniol 14th**

places of historic interest to occupy non-golfers while golfers strive to find their game at St. Deiniol, not least the pier, recently restored to its Victorian elegance, and Penrhyn Castle, an immense neo-Norman stately home which currently houses a doll museum and an industrial railway museum, but was in its time home to the Pennant family who owned the Penrhyn slate quarries in Bethesda.

As with numerous courses in North Wales the views are very extensive and take in Snowdonia and the Menai Straits. Those fine players, the Australian Norman Von Nida, Charlie Ward (that wizard of the short game), Ireland's Fred Daly (1947 Open Champion) and Bill Shankland (the Australian who was not only a superb golfer but also a Rugby League international) graced the fairways when they staged an exhibition match in the early '50s.

Braid's course remains the same in principle but various developments have evolved over the past 85 years. Many of these changes have been brought about by nature in the profusion of gorse and trees. The course, with its hilly and rugged terrain, is very exposed to the elements.

The opening hole, with its slightly low-lying tee, although not long, is far from a push-over with its acutely right-to-left sloping fairway. The 2nd hole, with its newly appointed medal tee, is set back in a spinney and can only be a nightmare for the habitual slicer due to the abundance of gorse, trees and heavy rough.

For me the next hole is one of the finest in North Wales. This subtle dog-leg left with its undulating fairway and pulpit green plays all of its 373 yards. The tee shot, played to an uphill, narrowing fairway, leaves a menacing second shot to be negotiated and, whatever club you think you should be using, I should recommend you use at least one club stronger.

The 4th, the first of six par-3s – and the longest – tends to play somewhat shorter than the card indicates because of a downhill, fast-running approach to the green. Out-of-bounds to the left and a deep line of trees to the right can make the tee shot on the 5th quite intimidating on this roller-coaster fairway. An average tee shot makes for a blind second to a small green which gathers the ball from the left.

The Stroke Index 1 6th has the same perils to the right as on the previous holes. With its precipitous fairway it seems interminable! Out-of-bounds is ominously close, being only a few paces through the back of the green. It is followed by back-to-back par-3s, the 7th and 8th, the first of them from a tee encircled by trees to a raised green and, without question, the trickier of the two. Across

the road is the new 8th tee. Because of the falling ground it is so easy to underclub to the large, sloping green. Approaching the half-way stage a short yet demanding par-4 awaits with its narrow uphill fairway and small rolling green that requires a dextrous putting touch.

The 10th, the fourth of the par-3s, is relatively straightforward and plays slightly downhill to a generously large, flat green. With yet more bushes and an abundance of rock outcrops the 11th has another sting in its tail: a blind second shot to the green. The right-hand side of the next hole is a definite *No Go* area due mainly to the numerous hazards as mentioned on earlier holes, while an awkwardly placed tree down the same side can easily foil the approach shot to the tricky undulating green.

If the 13th is the design of James Braid one has to question his sense of humour! What a card wrecker with its cocktail of hazards including out-of-bounds either side of the fairway and extensive masses of rocks and bushes. A twisting and turning uphill fairway makes a par score some achievement and a bogey cannot be frowned upon.

Standing on the 14th tee, which I have done many times over the years playing in 4-ball matches and with more concern about whether I was winning or losing a few bob, I have rarely taken the opportunity to stand and stare. It would appear that every roof top in the city of Bangor is visible from this the highest point on the course. An up-hill-and-down-dale zigzagging fairway which plummets down towards a large, low lying green makes for a testing par-5.

It is back across the road now to the short 15th with its lofty tee. Sticking to tradition that par-3s do not have fairways, this is a little gem with bushes positioned directly in front of the target. Given the opportunity to place three or four traps on this bunkerless course it would be around this green that they would go. Through the gate, across the lane and a minute's walk through woodland takes us to the picturesque 16th with its concave fairway and plateau green. It is probably the least taxing hole on the course.

The penultimate hole is played across a slight ravine where underclubbing could prove disastrous. The green, with its subtle slopes, should be treated with caution. The par-5 18th heads towards the clubhouse and has a wide open fairway in its early stages which then narrows considerably. A long line of trees on the left side could be troublesome. With a downhill approach to the green it should be noted that out-of-bounds lurks only a few paces

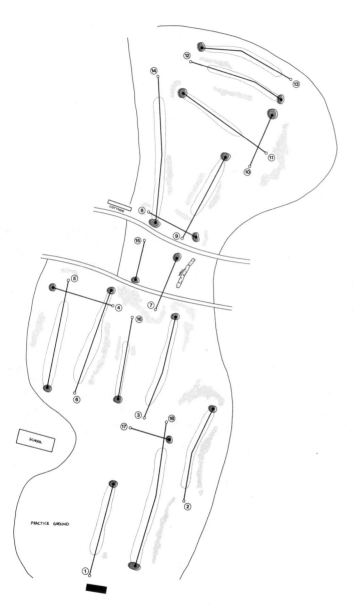

from the back of the green. With my round completed and a few moments to gather my thoughts, I could not help but agree with what I have so often heard said about this tough par-68 golf course: namely, if you can play to your handicap at St. Deiniol Golf Course you can play to it anywhere.

*(PL)*

### Card of the course:

| | | | | | | |
|---|---|---|---|---|---|---|
| 1. | 327 yards | par 4 | | 10. | 199 yards | par 3 |
| 2. | 352 | 4 | | 11. | 366 | 4 |
| 3. | 373 | 4 | | 12. | 347 | 4 |
| 4. | 233 | 3 | | 13. | 354 | 4 |
| 5. | 376 | 4 | | 14. | 528 | 5 |
| 6. | 398 | 4 | | 15. | 145 | 3 |
| 7. | 182 | 3 | | 16. | 315 | 4 |
| 8. | 198 | 3 | | 17. | 127 | 3 |
| 9. | 325 | 4 | | 18. | 512 | 5 |
| Out: | 2764 yards | par 33 | | | | |
| In: | 2893 yards | par 35 | | | | |
| Total: | 5657 yards | par 68 | | s.s.s. 67 | | |

# St. Melyd

*5839 yards; par 68; s.s.s. 68*

Hagiography is the preserve of the specialist when it comes to Celtic saints. Even the *Oxford Dictionary of Saints* misses out on St. Tudno, and as for St. Melyd he (or she?) might just as well be the Patron Saint of Lead Miners! As far as golf is concerned, the said Saint has chosen a lovely spot for recreation – on a warm May morning with the fir-clad mountain on one side and the blue sea on the other, whitewashed houses at either end of the course, one could have been in Provence. The Saint modestly demands no

**St. Melyd 3rd**

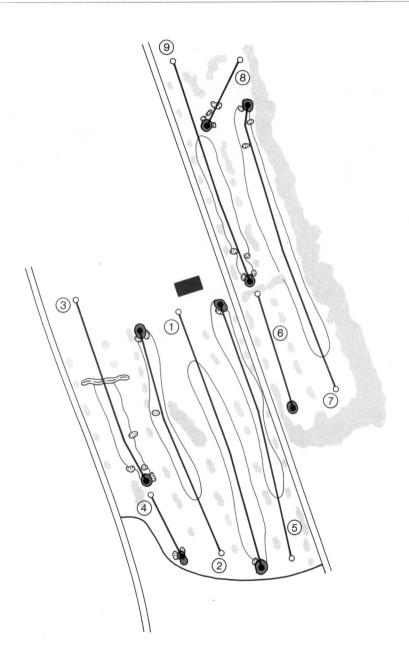

more than nine holes, but with alternative tees for each half a varied round of eighteen holes is offered, yardages altered somewhat and angles modified significantly.

The very first hole bears this out, a formidable par-4 played as the 1st and a bogey-5 when it occurs again as the 10th. The fairway leans to the right, descending gently on the drive and climbing correspondingly on the second shot. However you approach the green it will probably be without seeing the bottom of the flag. You may as well acclimatise yourself to this feature, for nearly all the greens here are raised sufficiently to present this problem. If you were wise you glanced at the 2nd green on your way past in order to ascertain where the hole has been cut, and as you play towards it you should gather what information you can about the pin positions on the 3rd and 4th greens. The 2nd, as it happens, is a cracker of a hole, a lovely drive down to the bottom of a hill followed by a steep pitch up the other side. Trees encroach first from the right and then from the left to tighten things considerably and there is a bunker placed in the fairway to spoil that really long drive for which we all strive and which happens when we least expect it. The green may be broad but it is very shallow, and all approach shots, from whatever range, must be inch-perfect.

The 3rd is every bit as attractive with a drive across a valley (a stream at the bottom waiting to catch the topped tee shot) and a delicate uphill pitch past trees on the right and bunkers on both sides to find the green. After the very short, uphill 4th to a triple-decked Mackenzie green, the 5th makes lengthy progress along a sloping fairway back to the clubhouse. As you essay your second shot you will be all too aware of the old railway track bed on the right, to which the green is very close. The 11th at Royal Troon is a hole on the flat. This is not, but the effect is similar.

The railway was once a mineral line up to Dyserth. Now it is a public footpath and it enters the mind again as the 6th is played. The hole is bunkerless and all it takes is a mid-iron (or long-iron second time round) lined on the front left of the green. Into the wind, however, much more club will be required by most of us. The wind, again, affects strategy on the 7th, with its sloping fairway directing weak shots first into trees or a hedge on the left and then into bunkers short of the green.

So far all holes have run parallel and the one exception is the 8th, a modest, downhill par-3 that ought to be a wedge but can take as much as a 4-iron in adverse conditions. This may be a parkland course but the wind is likely to be maritime. To finish the round there is a drive from a tee low down to a broad fairway followed by a longer approach shot than the card suggests to a well-bunkered green backed by tall firs.

*(MR)*

| Card of the course: | | | | | |
|---|---|---|---|---|---|
| 1. | 423 yards | par 4 | 10. | 451 yards | par 4 |
| 2. | 399 | 4 | 11. | 386 | 4 |
| 3. | 322 | 4 | 12. | 337 | 4 |
| 4. | 112 | 3 | 13. | 128 | 3 |
| 5. | 439 | 4 | 14. | 402 | 4 |
| 6. | 177 | 3 | 15. | 207 | 3 |
| 7. | 500 | 5 | 16. | 499 | 5 |
| 8. | 135 | 3 | 17. | 145 | 3 |
| 9. | 386 | 4 | 18. | 391 | 4 |
| Out: | 2893 yards | par 34 | | | |
| In: | 2946 yards | par 34 | | | |
| Total: | 5839 yards | par 68 | | s.s.s. 68 | |

# Silver Birch

*3002 yards; par 60*

**Silver Birch 8th**

As a visitor you arrive at a championship course along the North Wales coast and find that it is filled with a championship. You are a member of one of these clubs and have forgotten that the course is completely booked out. Perhaps you have given up the unequal struggle against the gorse bushes and sand dunes or the necessity for a handicap certificate. Happily, new courses are springing up within easy reach which, while hardly aspiring to championship status, will still give golfing satisfaction. They may appear, statistically, to be mere pitch-and-putt courses but you need the skills of an accomplished golfer to bring them to their knees. At Betwys-yn-Rhos you are only a few miles inland from Abergele yet you are already in hill country and, having paid your modest green fee at the village shop, you can prove that you are a 10-handicap player by going round in a gross 70! The hourly chiming of the church bell in the village will tell you if you have taken too long to prove your point.

The 1st at Silver Birch may be only 134 yards from tee to green but a gully and stream to be crossed and a hedge along the right are enough to induce uncharacteristic topping in many of us. The next excitement comes on the 3rd, credited with being a par-4 on the score card, but a 4- or 5-iron to a strong player. The only trouble is that the ravine has to be crossed again and there are trees to be negotiated. For many, though, it will be wise to treat this as a bogey-4.

Pitching to the 2nd, 4th, 5th, and 8th is a matter of good judgement of club given the rise and fall of the land, while the 9th needs a stout punch with a long iron and not the slightest trace of fade. The two genuine par-4s are left. Success on the 6th depends entirely on coping with the two large trees which narrow the fairway in driving range. You can go over them, round them, between them, but whatever you do avoid finishing behind them! Everyone will want to have a tilt at the 7th green, but it demands a straight carry over a hedge and ditch and the penalty for failure may well be repairing the greenhouse in the garden to the right.

By the time this book appears in print a number of new tees will have been brought into play giving alternative routes when playing a full 18 holes. In addition there are a couple of "novice tees" allowing the less skilled amongst the party to play from realistic teeing grounds while giving the experienced player something to think about.

*(MR)*

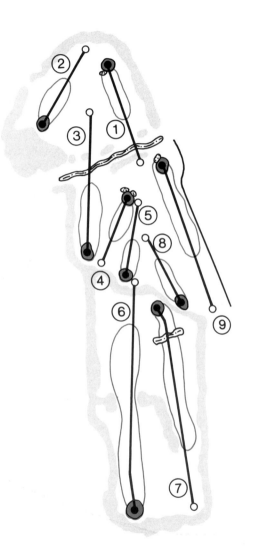

| Card of the course: | | |
|---|---|---|
| 1. | 134 yards | par 3 |
| 2. | 118 | 3 |
| 3. | 185 | 4 |
| 4. | 98 | 3 |
| 5. | 100 | 3 |
| 6. | 299 | 4 |
| 7. | 272 | 4 |
| 8. | 93 | 3 |
| 9. | 202 | 3 |
| Out: | 1501 yards | par 30 |
| Total: | 3002 yards | par 60 |

# Storws Wen

*5002 yards; par 68; s.s.s. 65*

Storws Wen on the Island of Anglesey was opened as recently as 23rd March 1996 and from the start it appears to have the ingredients for a winning formula. It is the brainchild of Mr. and Mrs. Ken Jones who wished to diversify from the agricultural use of this parcel of land which lies a couple of miles from the popular seaside town of Benllech where I spent many a childhood holiday. Three years of planning and hard work culminated in the official opening by Tony Lewis, one time England Cricket Captain, now television

**Storws Wen 1st**

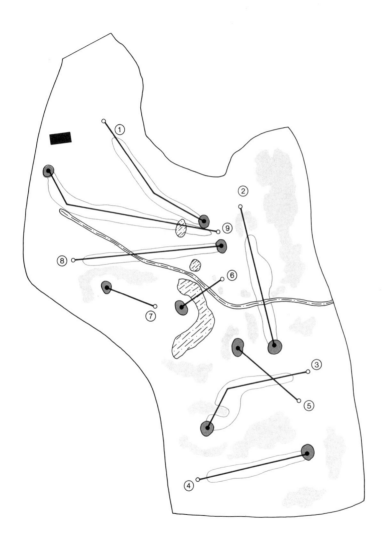

commentator and Chairman of the Wales Tourist Board, not to mention author of the foreword to this book. Teams of low handicap and scratch golfers then set about the course in an 18-hole stroke play event and, fittingly, the first course record of 67 was established by Clive Brown, Captain of the successful 1995 Walker Cup team, stalwart of golf in North Wales and valued contributor to our book.

The 1st hole is a subtle dog-leg left with out-of-bounds stretching the full length on the left. The fairway slopes left to right and the cleverly laid-out green slopes in the reverse. The high tee of the 2nd hole is the perfect invitation to be teased into doing all the wrong things. With bushes on both sides of the fairway and a ditch at a tantalising 215 yards out, the average golfer would be well advised to play short with a long- or mid-iron still allowing the player to see the green for the next shot. Even if you have the satisfaction of thumping the ball beyond the ditch a completely blind approach shot to the small green is far from advantageous.

There are two options on the 3rd drive. The more daring, a big shot with a wood, leaves only the shortest of pitches to the plateau green, the front of which consists wholly of rocky outcrops. The alternative is playing an iron from the tee leaving a much more daunting second shot, although there is an escape route provided to the left of the green. The length of the par-4s so far has been ever decreasing and the shortest comes next. The 4th appears innocuous enough on the score card but with out-of-bounds skirting the right side and bushes in wait on the left the hole is no push-over.

It pays to play the longest of the par-3s here with caution as out-of-bounds lies perilously close to the back of the green. It is followed by a grand little hole played from an elevated tee over a ditch and beautifully shaped lake crossed by an Augusta-style bridge. The two-tier green can cause much grief. Even shorter is the 7th but with bushes very close on the right the small green can be a difficult target to hit.

The emphasis is on a good tee shot on the 8th and there is no ducking the challenge of the ditch which runs almost the full length of the hole. More water comes into play on the 9th, the only par-5, in the form of a lake on the left of the fairway. With the hole dog-legging right and climbing steadily this is a testing final hole.

The greenkeeper and his staff should be congratulated on their achievements in such a short space of time. Their work, coupled with the sound design and the natural beauty of the scenery (with Snowdonia and the twin peak Rivals prominent in the distance) ensures that this course is bound to be immediately popular both with the locals and visiting golfers.

*(PL)*

### Card of the course:

| | | |
|---|---|---|
| 1. | 336 yards | par 4 |
| 2. | 334 | 4 |
| 3. | 302 | 4 |
| 4. | 271 | 4 |
| 5. | 188 | 3 |
| 6. | 113 | 3 |
| 7. | 108 | 3 |
| 8. | 357 | 4 |
| 9. | 492 | 5 |
| Out: | 2501 yards | par 34 |
| Total: | 5002 yards | par 68    s.s.s. 65 |

*Bob Hardy. Sec.*

# Vale of Llangollen

*6673 yards; par 72; s.s.s. 73*

The Oldest Member, parable teller to P. G. Wodehouse, was wont to sit where he could overlook the golf course and watch with fascination the duffers and foozlers who struggled "raggedly up the hill to the ninth green." He it was who had discovered "that perfect peace, that peace beyond all understanding, which comes at its maximum only to the man who has given up golf." Despite my erratic play I have not yet given up golf, but if I had a regular seat by the window in the clubhouse at the Vale of Llangollen Golf Club I could be tempted. It is a grand spot to rest while others toil for from it you can watch them on a very large part of the course.

*Vale of Llangollen 10th*

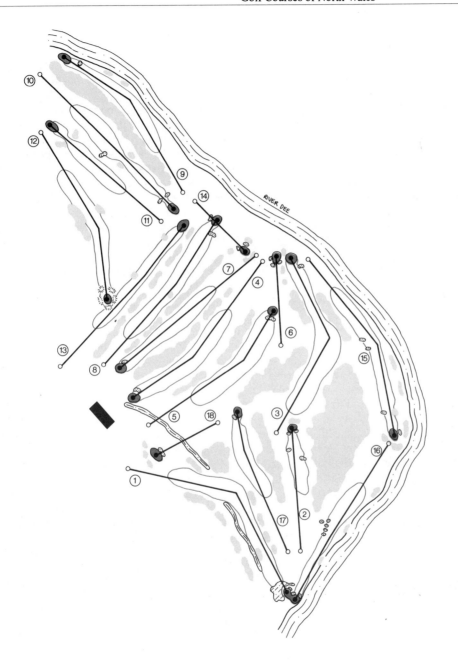

As a tourist centre Llangollen needs no introduction to the knowledgeable traveller. It has everything: a steam railway, horse drawn boats, a spectacular aqueduct, the ruined Dinas Bran, action holidays and activities, haunting Valle Crucis Abbey, museums and exhibitions of all kinds from Victorian school life to Dr. Who, Plas Newydd (home of the remarkable Eleanor Butler and Sarah Ponsonby, the Ladies of Llangollen), the world famous International Musical Eisteddfod, and one of the longer golf courses in this book. Surrounding Llangollen, and the golf course too, for that matter, are forested mountains and they provide a glorious backdrop for the River Dee as it winds its way towards Chester and the sea. The river forms the major boundary of the course and three splendid holes take full advantage of its handsome, if treacherous, company.

Perusal of the card shows that the length of the course comes partly from the fact that there are only three short holes but mainly from those par-4s which exceed 400 yards in length. Fortunately they are pretty flat and this is, then, one of those courses from which you can enjoy the mountains without having to climb them. I was told, before starting my round, that the course had evolved naturally over the years as new ground became available and that no specific architect had been involved. Whether I would have deduced this fact from closer study of the course as I first played it I cannot say, but natural evolution has provided a number of interesting challenges, architect or no architect. On meadowland turf many of these longer par-4s are going to be just out of reach of the average player and here the stars shine. Llangollen has its own star, its professional, David Vaughan. In his time he has been a World Cup player for Wales and has been selected for the prestigious PGA Cup team against the Americans.

The opening drive is exciting, whatever your standard of play. Good players should have no trouble reaching (or passing) the marker post down below in the distance, but until we have played a few holes the rest of us will be uncertain of our prospects and the threat of out-of-bounds on the right is very real as are the twin scourges of ditches on either side just where the fairway begins to bend right. Low handicappers may then be reminded of the 13th at Augusta (and not merely by the beauty of the setting) as they fret about whether or not they can carry the next little stream and its attendant pond just in front of the green. After a very short par-4 along an avenue of trees, the 3rd is another par-5 at the sort of length on which experts hope to pick up a stroke. It is a dog-leg to the left, the green bunkered in such a way that it favours those who risked cutting the corner.

The 4th is the first of a number of substantial two-shotters side by side in the middle of the course, working slightly right over a gentle rise before running in between trees and a bunker to the green. Another of those parallel holes, the 5th, is troubled by an internal out-of-bounds and there is a cross-bunker to test the accuracy of our pitching. Cross-bunkers thrive here and, uncompromising though they are, I was reminded as I encountered them that they are a traditional obstacle and their demise over the last twenty or thirty years is sometimes to be regretted. Dominating the hilltop in front is the ruin of Dinas Bran and the hole is appropriately named.

There is only a single par-3 on the way out, the 6th, and it plays between, or over, bunkers, depending on which of the tees is in use. A number of holes meet up here and though it could be hazardous if a large party of inaccurate visitors were present, it would be a good site for a table of drinks on a summer Saturday! The 7th leaves the spot and the 8th returns to it, the 7th more rolling than its companion (the 4th), and the 8th a strong hole with a tight drive between an out-of-bounds hedge on the left and a big tree right of the fairway. Judging the approach shot on the 8th, over a cross-bunker but stopping before plunging into the River Dee, adds to the fun.

A great deal more fun (or pain if you are prone to slicing) awaits on the 9th, the famous *River Hole*. It is utterly simple in its strategy: hit a decently long drive down the middle and set yourself up for a mid- to long-iron drawing in slightly to the green. There are complications! For a start the River Dee runs in a long arc on the right for the whole length of the fairway. Then there is a big bank topped with trees on the left which is bound to interfere with the first and second shots of those who aim away from the river. Even if you can see the green round to the left behind a shoulder of the bank as you play your second your troubles may not be over for the green appears to be friendly enough, perhaps even leaning away from the river, but hitting to it turns out to be akin to "pitching onto a policeman's helmet"[*].

The trees which topped the bank to the left of the *River Hole* threaten again on the 10th, but the aim is to split the twin oaks after which the hole is named and then pitch in between a pair of bunkers. At this point you think your troubles are all over. You relax and hope to saunter through the mundane looking meadowland 11th, Stroke 18, surely the easiest hole on the course. Its green looks flat enough...! Returning alongside, the drive at the 12th, *Bryn Dethol*, is one for the stalwart, tight between a big tree on the left and an out-of-bounds field on the right. The bunkerless green is ringed with mounds, a wonderfully archaic feature of the golf courses of my youth but rarely seen these days.

Around here you might think that the best is over, that the excitement of the river and its bank is a thing of the past. First get yourself through the strictures of the narrow 13th, then make sure you are not deceived on the short 14th, and only then essay the 15th. This is a short par-5, the sort of thing good golfers devour. They only devour it if they can constrain their drives in the neck of fairway as it bears right and ensure their second shots are unhindered by the right-hand bunker and left-hand tree. The rest of us pay rather greater attention to the proximity of the river omnipresent on the left.

[*] A remark first made about the 2nd at Royal Worlington and reported by Patric Dickinson but equally appropriate here.

Again the river preys on the mind of the ordinary golfer on the alluring 16th. It flows on the left, just beyond the fairway, from tee to green. If anything we drive away from it, but a cluster of five bunkers awaits us. Then we have to hit unerringly straight to find the green, shared with the 1st and separated from it by a couple of bunkers, with that glistening river only inches to the left. Word has it that these greens are to be fully separated, but come here in May or June, whatever the greens, and the hillside beyond is ablaze with Rhododendron and Azalea. Come here at any other time of the year and the golf is no less exacting. The gentle right-hand dog-leg of the 17th ought not to detain us, nor, according to the card, should the 18th, but the hole is uphill, the green is behind a cross-bunker and the putting surface is divided into two levels. Reading the slopes on a cross-putt here is the province of clairvoyants.

*(MR)*

### Card of the course:

| | | | | | |
|---|---|---|---|---|---|
| 1. | 486 yards | par 5 | 10. | 428 yards | par 4 |
| 2. | 288 | 4 | 11. | 334 | 4 |
| 3. | 498 | 5 | 12. | 403 | 4 |
| 4. | 425 | 4 | 13. | 425 | 4 |
| 5. | 387 | 4 | 14. | 158 | 3 |
| 6. | 189 | 3 | 15. | 489 | 5 |
| 7. | 391 | 4 | 16. | 410 | 4 |
| 8. | 410 | 4 | 17. | 362 | 4 |
| 9. | 425 | 4 | 18. | 165 | 3 |

| | | | | |
|---|---|---|---|---|
| Out: | 3499 yards | par 37 | | |
| In: | 3174 yards | par 35 | | |
| Total: | 6673 yards | par 72 | | s.s.s. 73 |

# Welsh Border Complex

*6012 yards; par 72; s.s.s. 69*

**Welsh Border Complex 3rd**

*The R&A's now-notorious 1987 report, The Demand for Golf, which called for some 700 new courses, was widely interpreted as a licence to print money. But as the golf dreamers conjured-up ever grander schemes against a background of* spiralling land prices, the bubble had to burst. Many painful lessons have been learned.[*]

These words appeared on my breakfast table the very day after I

---

[*] Dominic Pedler Golf World May 1996

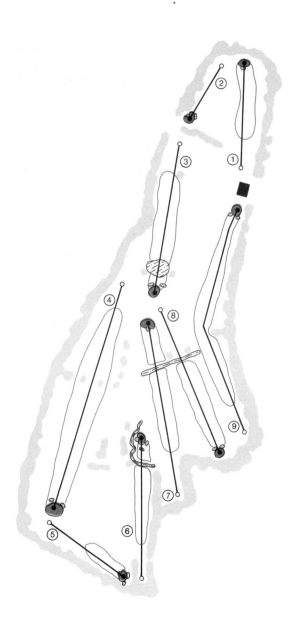

had sat in Roy Albinson's kitchen discussing, over a cup of tea, his golf course and his philosophy on running it. Quite simply he wants his golfing visitors to enjoy themselves and to want to come back. He could, for instance, have squeezed an 18-hole course onto his land, but he opted instead for 9 spaciously laid out holes on which it is almost impossible for golfers on one hole, however erratic their play, to interfere with those on another hole. He could keep the course open at all times and in all weathers to grab as many green fees as possible. If the course is not fit he closes it. In this way he satisfies his customers and ensures that his young golf course suffers no damage through short-term greed. Fortunately he has the additional facilities of a par-3 short course and a driving range on site.

If you can, take the minor road from Crew Green over the hills by Rodney's Pillar towards Middletown. I suspect you are actually in Shropshire here but as Bulthy Farm, where the course is situated, has a Welsh postal address its inclusion in this book causes me no problem. The views from the course are expansive, west far into Mid-Wales, south down the Vale of Powis past Long Mountain, and east towards Stiperstones and the Long Mynd. A great many trees have been planted which will add to the golfing strategy as the course matures, but for the moment most problems will be of the golfer's own making.

A short par-4 and gentle par-3 get you off to an amiable start, taking you round the back of the farm to the showpiece hole, the 3rd. The views southwards from the tee are broad but the eye is caught by the pond between two trees immediately in front of the green. You want to leave yourself a full shot over it but a hedge on the right eats into the fairway just waiting to catch the careless lay-up tee shot. On the 4th there are no difficulties as long as you do not contrive to leave your drive stuck behind one of the four trees crossing the fairway.

Most of us will aim left of the 5th green and hope that the slope will bring the ball in towards the flag, but this is Woosnam country (Lyle and Baker, too, for that matter) and perhaps we ought not to duck the challenge of the direct route over the green-front bunker. There is no great problem on the 6th drive, but the pitch is fun, over three bunkers to an L-shaped green on which on Feast Days the pin might be placed over to the left, behind one of the bunkers and precariously close to the stream. There is another stream to cross on the 7th but the real challenge is hitting the approach shot strongly enough to climb over the deep bunker in front of the ledge green. On the 8th you drive on the line of the Wrekin and to finish the round there is a telling drive pinched between a ditch on the left and a hedge on the right, the fairway then working to the right and slightly uphill alongside the road. This is not a slicer's course!

*(MR)*

### Card of the course:

| | | |
|---|---|---|
| 1. | 237 yards | par 4 |
| 2. | 142 | 3 |
| 3. | 339 | 4 |
| 4. | 520 | 5 |
| 5. | 201 | 3 |
| 6. | 317 | 4 |
| 7. | 385 | 4 |
| 8. | 344 | 4 |
| 9. | 521 | 5 |
| Out: | 3006 yards | par 36 |
| Total: | 6012 yards | par 72  s.s.s. 69 |

# *Welshpool*

*5708 yards; par 70; s.s.s. 69*

On a fair day with clouds racing their shadows across the unspoiled hill country of the Marches it matters, today, little whether you are in wild Montgomeryshire or Housman's Shropshire for they are each as blissfully detached from the commercial battles of Threadneedle Street as once they were the scene of some of the bloodiest fighting witnessed in our land. This is the gentle and pastoral, peaceful and radiant country of Offa's Dyke, to the east of which a Welshman would, once upon a time, on first being apprehended, lose his right hand, next time his life.

For many Englishmen Welshpool is the gateway to Mid-Wales. They come here to enjoy the architecture of Powis Castle, the artistic life of Gregynnog, the wines of one of the more enterprising independent provincial merchants still in business, and the delights of steam travel on the Welshpool and Llanfair Railway. Golfers should compulsorily be made to play Welshpool as an essential part of their golfing experience. Historians, too, ought to visit Welshpool's 4th green if only to speculate on what a difference to world history might have been made had one chief or other, Welsh or English, established a castle there, for there are few spots, even in this privileged part of the world, commanding such a strategic advantage. Those historians, too, could speculate on what might have been had James Braid been fortification consultant to either side, for he it was who revealed the potential of this site when laying out the course between the wars.

I came here first thirty years ago on a society outing with my father. We managed no more than half a dozen holes before we were driven off by torrential rain and howling winds – in mid-summer! On a warm day with a gentle breeze in early autumn it was a very different proposition, the views over a most extraordinary variety of hills and mountains incomparable, the gorse brilliant yellow, bracken russet, and the trees over adjacent hills every shade from the darkest of greens to the fieriest of reds. You are over 1,000 feet above sea level here, possibly not the highest golf in all Wales but not far off it, so if you have heart problems drive to the clubhouse, perch on the bench below the 18th green, watch the others playing, and leave it at that. As I made my notes I wrote "Heart stopping" about the view from the final tee. When I scaled the fairway on the far side of the valley I began to hope I had not been prophetic. This is strenuous golf, but if you have the constitution and game for it, your rewards will be many.

Beginning as the course means you to go on you strike out boldly up the steepest of hills and down the far side to find a plateau green not to be missed to left or right. The hole is named *Braid's Way* and already you are aware that names are of more value than yards in this alpine country. The 2nd is seemingly one of the less complicated holes as it is on flatter and lower ground but it is not easy with a wood encroaching threateningly from the right on the drive and a gully to be crossed with the next shot.

Yardages are totally irrelevant in trying to work out what club to take on the 3rd. Not only must you allow for the wind, ever present on these slopes, but also you need to add several clubs in order to climb the hill in front, foreshortened somewhat by the intervening gully. By now you will have realised that an apparently level green may well be far from it in such hilly country. This green turns out to be abundantly domed. On few courses, either, will the 4th stroke hole be a mere 297 yards, but then Welshpool is no place for preconceptions. The drive is not the problem, as long as you reach the fairway uphill over bracken. The real trial is in trying to pitch up to a pinnacle green, a task little easier than stopping a 7-iron on top of the Matterhorn, and, truth to tell, you may need even more than a 7-iron for your second shot when the wind is up.

At last the pressure is taken off with a succession of short par-4s of which full advantage should be taken, but even these involve vigorously sloping fairways on which it is absolutely essential to choose the precise line and hit it spot on. And then, down below the hillside, all is changed with an attractive par-3, the 8th, *Castle View*, set off by gorse on the left and bracken on the hill beyond. The prudent golfer tries not to leave a downhill putt on this treacherous green.

*Round the Bend* is the name of the 9th and that alone would be adequate description were it not for the fact that the hole climbs earnestly as it curves round the hillside, while the green is an extraordinary kidney-shaped affair on a plateau. Even from a forward winter tee and with a helpful following wind I still needed wood to make the green. Get the angles wrong and a big score looms.

The 10th was a cruel hole on which to be called through! It is not long, and I doubt my drive was any more than 50 yards from the green, but, having slogged up the hill trying not to hold up my benefactors, I was incapable of pitching 5 yards let alone 50. It is as imperative to pace the body and golf round here as it is through 7,500 yards of Florida swamp in mid-July.

Happily, a rest is available on top of the moors as an attempt is made to drive the green on the 11th and only an artificial out-of-bounds inhibits the fullest of shoulder turns on the 12th, *The Fort*. Yet this is the 2nd Stroke Hole and as the approach is played to the green the reason is made plainly apparent. The golfer is required to miss neither to left nor to right nor through the back for the green stands aloof above an all-consuming abyss. What makes the shot so difficult is judging the effect of the downhill run in to the putting surface and the wind is bound to have a hand in things as well. The 13th, *Llanfair Ginny*, is another brief respite, and this is further chance to take in the magnificent panoramas and fill the lungs with the freshest of air.

There are not many par-3 holes accorded the status of Stroke 3. The 14th at Welshpool is one of them. Each short hole here is full of character and if you crack a precise mid-iron over the valley and steeply up past a bunker to hold the left-to-right green you will reckon the 14th is a corker. If you miss on the right your contribu-

***Welshpool 8th***

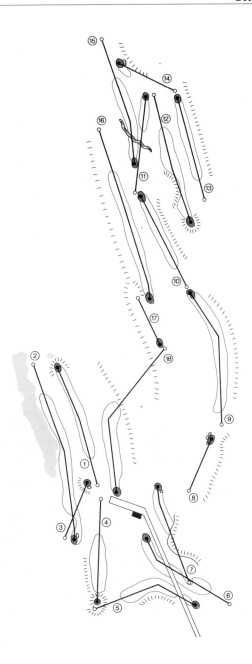

tions to the swear-box will be generous. In theory the 15th provides another breather as long as you to not tangle with the gorse on the right which gives the hole its name or the ditch which crosses the fairway short of the green.

The 16th and 17th take you to the other side of the hill which has dominated your life since the 9th. The views on this side of the hill are every bit as noble as those on the other. Neither is a hole on which to develop a slice and the 17th's name, *Old Nick*, warns that a lapse of concentration could be costly.

As you approach this 17th green the awfulness of your situation becomes apparent. Here you are on one mountain and there, half a mile away, on another mountain, is the clubhouse. On the far side of the intervening deep valley is a fairway first climbing straight and then bending sharply left as it continues to rise towards the green. There is a marker post something like 250 yards from the 18th tee so it is in theory reachable in ideal conditions but that implies a carry of the order of 240 yards. If you hit less powerfully (and most of us do) try to assess just how much you dare bite off and you will get no marks for crashing into the bracken trying to play too conservatively. Put this hole down with such classics as the 1st at Macrihanish or 5th at Mid-Ocean. This is a *Cape Hole* of the first order and, debilitating though it may be to walk it, cause enough to visit Welshpool even if it were not for its seventeen uplifting precursors.

*(MR)*

| Card of the course: | | | | | |
|---|---|---|---|---|---|
| 1. | 347 yards | par 4 | 10. | 295 yards | par 4 |
| 2. | 497 | 5 | 11. | 275 | 4 |
| 3. | 169 | 3 | 12. | 376 | 4 |
| 4. | 297 | 4 | 13. | 297 | 4 |
| 5. | 322 | 4 | 14. | 185 | 3 |
| 6. | 317 | 4 | 15. | 363 | 4 |
| 7. | 297 | 4 | 16. | 503 | 5 |
| 8. | 159 | 3 | 17. | 150 | 3 |
| 9. | 402 | 4 | 18. | 457 | 4 |
| Out: | 2807 yards | par 35 | | | |
| In: | 2901 yards | par 35 | | | |
| Total: | 5708 yards | par 70 | | s.s.s. 69 | |

# Wepre Park

*2788 yards; par 54*

How is your iron play? I thought mine was in reasonable shape until it was thoroughly examined by Wepre Park. I am ashamed to say that if I had not been writing this book I would not have given it a thought, assuming it was just a glorified pitch-and-putt course.

It is a municipal facility of a kind of which we in Cheshire are desperately short, a serious par-3 course of the most interesting kind, and a good test for golfers of all abilities.

If you are a left-hander leave your slice at home! There is

**Wepre Park 4th**

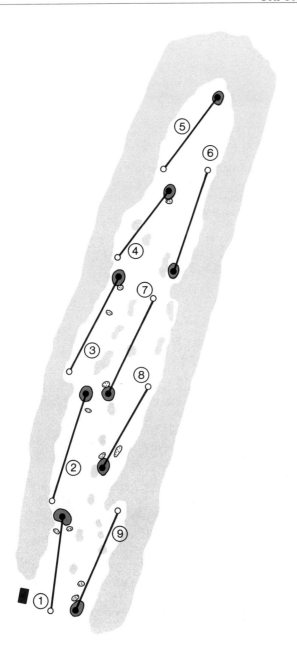

trouble on the left of every hole and it is plainly evident on the 1st on which it is possible to hide the flag round the corner to the left behind bushes. Already we are climbing and on the 2nd you will be doing well if you can reach the green at all with an iron, and the 3rd is hardly less demanding. Even the short 4th plays much longer than the card suggests particularly when the wind gets up. It is a delight, all carry across a gully. After the little 5th played down into a corner the 6th begins the run home, an attractive target in its own encircling moundwork. The last three holes tumble downhill and on each it is wise to aim right of the flag and let the slope bring the ball round. Err to the left on any of them and you are likely to find yourself searching in the woods far below to find the ball. The 9th, played out of those woods, needs height to clear a tree growing directly in line with the green.

*(MR)*

**Card of the course:**

| | | |
|---|---|---|
| 1. | 151 yards | par 3 |
| 2. | 184 | 3 |
| 3. | 182 | 3 |
| 4. | 93 | 3 |
| 5. | 113 | 3 |
| 6. | 173 | 3 |
| 7. | 173 | 3 |
| 8. | 161 | 3 |
| 9. | 164 | 3 |
| Out: | 1394 yards | par 27 |
| Total: | 2788 yards | par 54 |

# Wrexham

*6233 yards; par 70; s.s.s. 70*

Wrexham's hosting of the 1995 Ladies' Home Internationals confirmed what players in the British Senior Ladies Championships and many a national championship, too, will have thought: that Wrexham is a good all round test of golf. There is a welcome variety to the lengths of the holes; it is not a succession of long par-4s of the sort that average players will never reach even with two wooden shots; and, as many a visitor remarks having played the course, no two holes are alike. As you drive in you cross the

**Wrexham 4th**

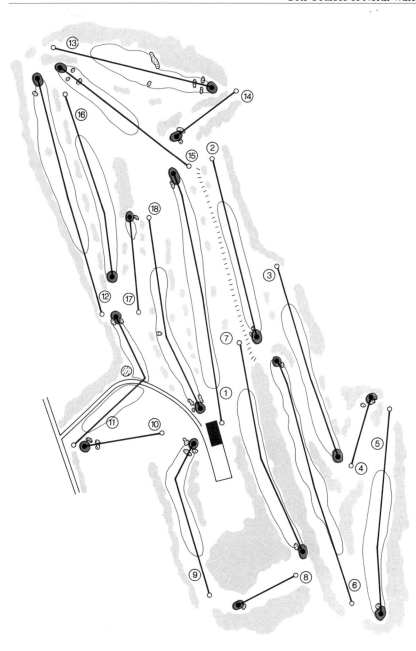

11th fairway yet you still have no idea of what the course will be like. From here it looks like flattish, gentle parkland. It is anything but!

The club was founded back in 1906 and it moved to its present home in 1923 when James Braid was engaged to lay out the course. This remained intact until, during World War II, runways from Borras Aerodrome ate into parts of it. Alterations were made when the course was resurrected in peacetime and the extent of those alterations can be ascertained from close study of the two course maps hanging outside the Secretary's office. You will not be aware of who built exactly what as you play, but you will hardly fail to notice the influence of Braid all the way round, the bunkers in particular displaying more vigour and variety than is common in this part of Wales. (That said, there is also impressive bunkering to be found at Prestatyn and both courses join together annually to host the 72-hole Clwyd Championship.) The greens, too, are full of slopes and borrows and, with much of the course on gently rolling higher ground, the wind will usually need to be considered. Extensive quarrying in the vicinity suggests that drainage will be good and so it is, much of the turf heathland in character and the greens firm, demanding confidence with the pitch shot.

Standing on the 1st tee you are encouraged to go for a big drive, the fairway running away gently down a valley before climbing over the last few yards to a ledge green high above a prominent bunker. Up above, the 2nd doubles back and you are conscious of both the hedge running down the left and the big drop just off the fairway to the right, the pitch needing to be hit precisely to find the correct level on this stepped green. The drive at the 3rd seems tighter still, squeezed between a line of trees on the left and a group on the right, protecting the 6th green. The approach here is made downhill over bumpy ground and it is said that the easier route in is from the left, but even so the pitch can be difficult to hold on this green.

The Captain told me that even in a social match no putt is ever conceded on the 4th with its sloping, banana-shaped green beyond two bunkers and surrounded by trees. I can understand why! It is a pretty hole, though, and is followed by a very strong par-4, the 5th. Positioning of the drive is important here, for the fairway slopes from left to right and you will want to try to ensure a level stance for the second shot, up over a ridge towards the green. Many approaches will be made from the lower, right side of the fairway and then the devilishly placed bunker, front right of the green, is sure to enter play. The views from this part of the course are expansive, and the prospect from the 6th tee is thrilling. Unfolding before you is a tumbling and twisting fairway rolling in waves as it descends. But then it climbs again and it will always take a couple more clubs to reach the green than you think! Off to the left of the fairway there is trouble aplenty in the woods around which the 7th curves insistently. It is a tough hole from the yellow tee – and unthinkable from the medal tee 85 yards further back. As well as bending, the fairway slopes mischievously from right to left and you may find it necessary to take aim on the right-hand edge of the fairway with the drive in order to ensure that your second shot is not cut off by trees. The green is raised up above a bunker and tucked away round the corner, no easy target even after a perfect drive.

A delightful short hole, the 8th, is played to a ledge green in a woodland corner and then, again, there is a big difference between yellow and white tees on the 9th. From whichever tee you play, however, the strategy has to be similar: aim for position on the bend where the fairway turns sharp right and pitch in over gloriously heaving bunkers to find the green.

The back nine ought to be easier, for it is nearly 500 yards shorter but, as we all know, golf just is not like that! There should be no problem at all on the short 10th, but the bunkers simply have to be carried. The 11th is really only a drive and pitch, yet if you intend to play it that way you have to take on the challenge of an out-of-bounds along the left-hand side. If you play too conservatively from the tee the green, between bunkers and close to a hedge, will not be quite so easy to find.

Each of the par-5s here runs in the same direction, so if one is out of range of two big shots they all are! The drive at the 12th has to be placed in the right half of a narrow fairway with trees on both sides, the reason being obvious enough from the tee, for there is a big tree standing on the direct route to the green. It might be profitable to take a look over the brow of the hill before teeing off on the 13th as there is plenty of trouble on the left and you may prefer to lay up short of the gully over which the second shot is played to a green up behind three gaping bunkers. The 14th is yet another attractive short hole, the green guarded, it would seem, only by two bunkers, but watching play here for a short time (while I was waiting on the 2nd tee) it was educative to observe just how many different ways people found to make the hole difficult!

After a welcoming drive across a valley, bunkers are again the only trouble in front of the 15th green. Then the 16th may be bunkerless but it *is* the 4th stroke hole. It does no more than bend gently to the right but if you slice your drive you risk being out-of-bounds on the 12th fairway, and if you do not slice it you may find the ball charging away down a bank on the left having run out of fairway! Nor is a slice advised on the 17th, the ground, and putting surface, leaning down to the right. The round ends with a big drive, slightly uphill, to find the gap between trees on the left and a fairway bunker on the right. The approach, from some distance for most of us, must be made between big bunkers on either side of the final green.

*(MR)*

### Card of the course:

| | | | | | |
|---|---|---|---|---|---|
| 1. | 523 yards | par 5 | 10. | 171 yards | par 3 |
| 2. | 387 | 4 | 11. | 354 | 4 |
| 3. | 422 | 4 | 12. | 504 | 5 |
| 4. | 147 | 3 | 13. | 352 | 4 |
| 5. | 428 | 4 | 14. | 160 | 3 |
| 6. | 519 | 5 | 15. | 335 | 4 |
| 7. | 458 | 4 | 16. | 380 | 4 |
| 8. | 138 | 3 | 17. | 199 | 3 |
| 9. | 336 | 4 | 18. | 420 | 4 |
| Out: | 3358 yards | par 36 | | | |
| In: | 2875 yards | par 34 | | | |
| Total: | 6233 yards | par 70 | | s.s.s. 70 | |

# The Architects

It has to be said that few British golfers have the slightest clue who may have designed the course they play regularly. In many cases the courses of North Wales have evolved naturally and no specific architect can be credited other than God and a succession of Greens Committees. Below are details of the small number of architects we have been able to identify.

## Peter Alliss

Son of Percy Alliss, himself one of the finest European professionals in the inter-war years, Peter was a leading tournament player in the 1950s and '60s, playing in eight Ryder Cup teams, and winning Spanish (three times), Italian and Portuguese Opens in addition to many British trophies. As the principal British television commentator he is the natural successor to Henry Longhurst. His many commercial golfing enterprises include course design and construction, of which The Belfry (in partnership with David Thomas) is the most prominent.

## James Braid

One of "The Great Triumvirate" (with J.H. Taylor and Harry Vardon) who dominated golf in the first twenty years of this century, he won the Open Championship five times between 1901 and 1910. He was subsequently in great demand as an architect but, as he suffered from travel sickness, entrusted much of his on-site work to John R. Stutt who himself became an architect of note.

## Neil Coles

As well as being one of the most competitive British professionals of the '60s and '70s Coles has remained in the forefront of the professional game ever since, both as a participant in the Senior Tour and as Chairman of the PGA European Tour. In his work as a course architect he has been associated with a number of the new PGA stadium courses across the country.

## Collins Family

Sadly the authors have been unable to obtain biographies of Fred and Sid Collins, whose influence in golf course design in North Wales has been considerable. The authors would be most grateful for information for inclusion in later printings of this book.

## Harry Colt

Colt, born in 1869, was a Cambridge law graduate. He is reckoned to have been the first designer not to come from the professional ranks, the first to use the drawing board, the first to prepare plans for tree planting, and, most significantly, the first international designer. In creating Sunningdale effectively he moved golf inland.

## Herbert Fowler

Fowler did not even take up golf until he was 35 (in 1891), yet rapidly became a scratch amateur. In the early 1900s he designed and built what we now call the Old Course at Walton Heath (at the request of his brother-in-law whose consortium financed the project). It received immense critical acclaim and led to his partnership with the equally distinguished Tom Simpson in a design and construction company. Saunton, the New Course at Walton Heath, and the Berkshire are amongst the better-known of his other British courses.

# Hawtree Family

Three generations of Hawtrees, F.G., F.W., and M.G., have maintained this is as probably the longest continuous practice in golf course architecture since 1912. The jewel in the family's crown is undoubtedly Royal Birkdale as laid out by F.G. in 1932, further updated by F.W. in the '70s, the greens remodelled in 1993 by M.G. Internationally the firm has worked on courses from the United States to Iran, Japan to Turkey, and recent European Tour events have been played over their courses at Royal Waterloo, St. Nom-la-Brêteche and Pals. Many courses in North Wales have Hawtree connections, from a complete design down to maintenance advice, and it is their work in tight corners on restricted sites which demonstrates the value of employing a professional architect rather than the well-meaning, but less able amateur, Greens Committees.

# Harold Hilton

Hilton won the Open Championship as an amateur twice in the 1890s, the Amateur Championship four times, and was still competitive enough to win the U.S. Amateur at the Apawamis Club, New York, in 1911. His fellow member of the Royal Liverpool Club, John Ball, was the first Englishman to win the Open Championship, and both contributed substantially to the renown of this famous club. Its influence over the game in North Wales in the period before the First World War was considerable, not least in the layout of the early courses in which Hilton was frequently a consultant.

# Brian Huggett

Third in the 1962 Open Championship and runner-up in 1965, Huggett was one of the most tenacious players on the European circuit in the 1960s and '70s. He represented Wales in the World Cup no fewer than nine times and played in six Ryder Cups, perhaps his finest moment being an emotional halved match with Billy Casper in the famous tied match of 1969 at Royal Birkdale.

# John Jacobs

John Jacobs is probably better known for his long career as a world-wide authority on the teaching of golf, and therefore it is not generally known that he has been involved in golf course architecture for many years, designing courses as far away as Pakistan. In the recent past he has designed The Buckinghamshire, the Edinburgh Course at Wentworth and Aprémont just outside Paris, all courses which have received much acclaim. He is delighted with the outcome of his design at Northop Country Park one of the very few contemporary layouts in North Wales.

# Tom Jones

The Llandudno (Maesdu) course as we know it today was designed and built by the club's first professional, Tom W. Jones. Tom Jones turned professional in 1910 when he was appointed Club Professional to the Morfa Nefyn Golf Club. He then moved to the Llandudno Great Orme club where his brother, Cradoc, was assistant. Appointed to Maesdu as Professional in 1915 Tom Jones remained in that position until his death in 1967. During this period he played for, and captained, Wales in the first professional Home International series in 1938. He was appointed Captain of the PGA in 1957, the year that Great Britain and Ireland won the Ryder Cup at Lindrick, and later became Chairman of the PGA (1963-7). He was honoured by his club with Life Membership in 1938 and in 1962 he became the first professional to be honoured with the Captaincy of his club.

# Morris Family

It is difficult to ascertain exactly which Morris is responsible for which course in North Wales. "Old Tom" is credited with a good deal of work for which he cannot have been accountable. Some may have been done by his elder brother, George, who laid out the original 9-hole course at Hoylake. His son, Jack, became Professional at Royal Liverpool, teaching a little, playing a bit, and profitably making balls for customers in Scotland a good deal. "Old Tom" won the Open Championship in 1861, '62, '64 and '67 by which time he had returned to St. Andrews as greenkeeper and professional. It must be remembered that golf architecture in those days involved using as many of the natural features as possible. For instance, in the Royal Liverpool rules of 1869 it is stated that "No ball shall be teed less than six club lengths nor more than ten lengths from the hole". Teeing grounds consisted of an inch or two of sand scooped from the bottom of the hole...

## Donald Steel

Though one of the busiest architects of our time, Steel's influence in North Wales has been confined mainly to advice on amendments and refurbishments to courses rather than rebuilds or entirely new layouts. As adviser to the Royal and Ancient he has supervised alterations to Royal St. George's, Turnberry, Muirfield, Royal Birkdale and Royal Lytham in preparation for Open Championships. Golf correspondent to *The Sunday Telegraph* for nearly 30 years, he is also author of a number of authoritative golf books.

## David Thomas

After an impressive career as a tournament player (2nd twice in the Open Championship, winner of three Opens in Europe) Thomas began in course design with Peter Alliss. Their joint efforts included The Belfry, host to three Ryder Cups.

## Harry Vardon

Arguably the greatest of "The Great Triumvirate", Vardon's record of six wins between 1896 and 1914 in the Open Championship has not, of 1996, been equalled. He was also the first overseas winner of the U.S. Open (at Chicago in 1900). Though he did not invent it, his name is given to the grip in which the little finger of the right hand overlaps the first finger of the left, a grip used to this day by most golfers at all levels of competence. His style of play, more upright and less of a lunge than his contemporaries, showed that rhythm, balance and timing could be more effective than brute strength, particularly with the temperamental "gutty" ball.

## Other titles of interest from:

## SNOWDONIA ROCKY RAMBLES: Geology beneath your feet

### Bryan Lynas

This splendid guidebook is a revelation for all who have an interest in the countryside and why it looks the way it does. Read about the now-extinct massive volcanoes, the huge earth movements and glaciers that shaped this pleasant land. Discover birdlife, plants and fungi in the company of earth scientist and ecologist Bryan Lynas. The book is profusely illustrated with original sketches, detailed maps and informative photographs.

*"The walks alone will satisfy but, for those like me with a wish to know the Earth better, it opens the mind's eye to the form and structure of the land" – James Lovelock FRS (originator of The Gaia Hypothesis)*

*(£9.95)*

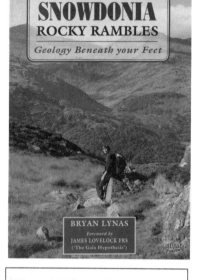

## WALKS IN MYSTERIOUS WALES

### Laurence Main

Follow the spirit paths of Wales - visit the most sacred and secret sites and discover the ancient traditions of this historic country in the company of a leading expert. And, while you're discovering Welsh heritage, enjoy some excellent walks across the length and breadth of the country.

Laurence Main has been involved in the longest-running research programme into the paranormal and some results of this unusual study are revealed for the first time in this book.

*(£6.95)*

**We publish books on walking, cycling, sport, heritage and cookery. For a free catalogue, please write to:**

**Sigma Leisure, 1 South Oak Lane, Wilmslow, Cheshire SK9 6AR. Or visit our web site at: sigmapress@zetnet.co.uk**

**Phone: 01625-531035; Fax: 01625-536800;**

**E-mail: sigma.press@zetnet.co.uk**

**ACCESS and VISA orders welcome – 24 hour Answerphone service! Most orders are despatched on the day we receive your order – you could be enjoying our books in just a couple of days. Please add £2 p&p to all orders.**